# <u>McFly Goes to Med School:</u>
## *Your Physician in the Unraveling U.S. Healthcare Crisis*

*Solutions for America's 47 million Uninsured*

## By Cecil Bennett, MD DABFP

authorHOUSE®

AuthorHouse™
1663 Liberty Drive, Suite 200
Bloomington, IN 47403
www.authorhouse.com
Phone: 1-800-839-8640

First published by AuthorHouse  5/20/2008

ISBN: 978-1-4343-8353-2 (e)
ISBN: 978-1-4343-8352-5 (sc)

Printed in the United States of America
Bloomington, Indiana

This book is printed on acid-free paper.

# TABLE OF CONTENTS

Introduction                                                    vii

CHAPTER I
**BLUE-COLLAR AMERICA**
**The Average Joe**                                               1

CHAPTER II
**THE MEDICAL STUDENT**
**The Glorified First-Round Draft Pick**                        11

CHAPTER III
**INTERNSHIP**
**A Living Hell**                                               23

CHAPTER IV
**MEDICAL RESIDENCY**
**Tragic Memories for a Lifetime**                              29

CHAPTER V
**THE PRACTICING PHYSICIAN**
**McFly Becomes the Point Guard**                               37

CHAPTER VI
**HOSPITALS**
**Cost-Containment to the Death**                               51

CHAPTER VII
**PHARMACEUTICAL AND HEALTH INSURANCE COMPANIES**
**WWE Tag Team Wrestling at Its Best**                          61

CHAPTER VIII
**MEDICAL EDUCATION Part 1**
**America Will Need a Lot More Doctors**                        71

CHAPTER IX
**MEDICAL EDUCATION Part 2**
Time to Think Outside the Box                                    81

CHAPTER X
**PRIMARY CARE AND MINORITY PHYSICIANS**
We Need Help—Today                                               93

CHAPTER XI
**EVERYONE HAS A RIGHT TO PROPER HEALTHCARE**
People Are People                                               103

CHAPTER XII
**THE BENNETT PLAN FOR THE U.S. HEALTHCARE SYSTEM**
Politics, Power Brokers, Prevention, Preparation,
and Partnership                                                 117

CHAPTER XIII
**THERE ARE A LOT OF DECISIONS TO BE MADE**
It's All up to You, McFly                                       135

110th Congress: House of Representatives                        145

110th Congress: Senate                                          191

References                                                      203

# Introduction

I am a family physician. I decided to write this book a couple years ago, after looking in the pantry closet and seeing five different kinds of cereal on one of the shelves. There was a box for every member of the family. I had several thoughts at that moment. I remembered when I was a child; my mother would take my sister and me to the supermarket, where we would spend a ridiculous amount of time in the cereal section arguing with each other about which one box of cereal we would get. One box was all my parents could afford. My mother was a bookkeeper and my father a plumber's assistant.

Now there were five boxes of cereal in my kitchen cupboard. I also thought of all the families that struggle with putting food on the table and fathers who dread the thought of their child or their wife getting sick and not having health insurance. I have lived hand to mouth. I have struggled to pay my mortgage. I have received government assistance of milk vouchers for my first child. Nothing scared me more than the time I spent without health insurance for my family. If you or your loved one got gravely ill, what else in life really would matter? What are people willing to pay to live? Health insurance is a right for all Americans. I see in my practice what happens to those without it.

There is so much more the public does not know regarding the pending crisis in healthcare on several critical fronts. People are going to die unnecessarily. The medical education system is going to implode. Costs are going to continue to go up exponentially if we do not act. I have attempted to write a book making the point person, the physician, real in this evolving monster called the U.S. healthcare system. Who really is this person you call your doctor?

In the hilarious movie *Back to the Future*, we meet a loveable character named George McFly who cannot get out of his own way. Bully Biff Tannen consistently dumps upon him. No matter how many wedgies or other forms of public humiliation George suffers at the hands of Biff, McFly just grins and bears it. For the last two decades in our society, physicians have played the role of McFly to Academy Award winning levels, while insurance companies, the government, lawyers, and drug companies have played the role of Biff on speed. The public is desperately waiting for Dr. McFly, its reluctant hero, to step up and take charge of healthcare. Essentially nothing starts in this $2-trillion-a-year industry called healthcare without a physician writing a prescription, ordering a test, or admitting a patient to the hospital, yet one would be hard pressed to find more impotent leadership than the leadership currently displayed by physicians. How did it get to this? Who is your doctor? What process made him what he is today? What will it take to wake this sleeping giant? These are but some of the questions that will be answered.

There are 47 million Americans without healthcare coverage and therefore without a voice. They are our neighbors, our barbers and hairdressers, our cleaners, our grocers. It is absolutely appalling that in one of the richest countries in the world 16 percent of the population is without health insurance. Recent studies indicate an increased rate of morbidity and mortality among the uninsured. Both my parents died young of diseases that were preventable. There is no greater issue facing an uninsured American today than the lack of health insurance. It is a greater issue than the economy. It is a greater issue than the war. It is a greater issue than immigration.

There is an opportunity here, and if physicians and the uninsured could understand each other and work together, a powerful alliance would be forged—an alliance that could completely overhaul healthcare in America. This book brings to life the mindset of the physician, the medical education system, and other key players in healthcare, with plenty of frank and sobering revelations. I also provide exciting new solutions to fix our broken healthcare system in all key areas—solutions that include providing $100 billion in annual health insurance premium coverage for all uninsured Americans, without raising individual income taxes. It is time for physicians and the uninsured to step up and make these solutions a reality.

This book explores areas in healthcare that no one wants to speak about. This book uncovers the secrets government, medical academia, hospitals, and drug companies do not want to address. I defy anyone to pick any chapter randomly, read it, and not come away shocked, confused, angry, frightened, or enlightened. The uninsured who act on the suggestions made in this book could decide the next presidential election and congress. The ideas in this book could revolutionize medicine for generations.

# CHAPTER I
# BLUE-COLLAR AMERICA
## The Average Joe

Most Americans are blue-collar, roll-up-our-sleeves, conservative-valued, god-fearing individuals. Despite what we may see every day on the local news, most of America is not New York, Los Angeles, Miami, or Chicago. Most of America is small towns that you have never heard of. These are places where people say good morning to you when they pass you on the street, whether or not they know you. They are small towns where, when you enter a store, someone with a genuine smile genuinely wants to help you—communities that support the local high school sport teams.

To individuals everywhere the thing that matters most is the future of our children. There is no greater priority. That is the reason we go to work each day. That is the reason we encourage our children to get as much education as possible. That is the reason we put off meeting our own personal needs. I have three small children: Daniel, thirteen; Matthew, eleven; and Allyssa, four. Most of the decisions my wife, Andrea, and I make on a daily basis revolve around the impact they have on our family.

I remember once when we attended a marriage seminar and one of the tasks we had to complete was a list of the ten things that were most important to us. The first and most important priority on each of our lists was our children. Our relationship with each other came second to our relationship with our children. That may be controversial to some, but that is the way we feel. I believe our priorities are the same as the priorities of any other American family.

Andrea and I find that our priorities concerning our children are no different from the perspective that our own parents had when it came to raising us. With that said, one can imagine how difficult it is for families that have no health insurance. These families not only have to wrestle with the daily struggle to put food on the table and keep a roof over their heads, but they also live with the fear that one of them—or even worse, one of their children—might get sick.

Lack of access not only means being unable to find a doctor or hospital to go to but also not knowing how to negotiate one's way through the cumbersome process of finding the *right* healthcare solution to one's problem, or again, even worse, your child's health problem. The issue of lack of knowledge in negotiating the healthcare system is very close to me. My mother died of colon cancer when she was forty-two. I was fourteen years old. My father died twelve years later of a preventable stroke. Their stories and situations are very similar to what blue-collar Americans face every day regarding healthcare.

My mother and my father migrated to the United States from Jamaica in the late '60s. My mother, with a high-school education, became a bookkeeper. My father, who left school after the third grade to help support his family, became a plumber's assistant. He eventually developed the experience to be a licensed plumber, but because of his limited education, he was unsuccessful in passing the examinations necessary. For his entire life, he was the one who did the work and the licensed plumber collected the money.

We lived in a rented apartment in Brooklyn, New York. My mother and my father aspired to one day save enough money to buy a home for their family. All those plans changed when in February 1979 my mother sat my younger sister and myself down and told us that she had cancer. Shortly after that conversation with our mother, our aunt, who is a nurse, sat my sister and me down again and informed us that my mother would not have more than three months to live. As young as we were, it was an incomprehensible situation and one we refused to believe.

My mother, not believing she could get the treatment that she needed in the United States (not unlike many cancer victims), went abroad to seek any other experimental treatments that could possibly save her life. She went to the Bahamas for such treatment.

For the first two months or so after our mother told us about her cancer, we rarely saw her because of her treatment schedule in the Bahamas. We prayed, though, that she would come back to us cured. Ultimately the treatment in the Bahamas did not do any good. I remember my father telling me how shocked he was when he got to the airport to pick her up and she exited Customs in a wheelchair. Her disease had weakened her to the point that she collapsed in the terminal and needed medical attendance.

For the next month, my mother laid in her bed at home. Various members of her church and family came every day to pray for her. I remember that the weaker she got, the more her abdomen swelled from the fluid that was accumulating there. I cannot imagine what was going through her mind during her last few weeks. There she was, forty-two years old (younger than I am at the time of this writing), knowing she would be leaving two small children and a husband who depended on her to do everything. She eventually died a few weeks later in a hospital in Brooklyn—in about the same period of time our aunt told us she would.

I am not certain of the screening tools that were available to the average citizen back in 1979. I don't even know if tools used today for colon cancer screening, such as a colonoscopy or fecal occult blood testing (testing the stool for hidden blood), existed in the late '70s. Even if they did exist, it would be unlikely that my mother would have been aware of them.

My mother's experience made me very sensitive to individuals today who *can* be screened for colon cancer but, because of a lack of information, a lack of knowledge, or even out of fear, are not tested. With the modern screening tools available, no one in this country should die of colon cancer. I believe most Americans do not know the circumstances or the symptoms that should immediately send them to a physician (whether or not they have insurance) to be screened for colon cancer.

Insured Americans at least have the option of going to a physician if they believe they are experiencing symptoms of cancer. Uninsured Americans more times than not take the position of doing nothing, hoping for a positive outcome, hoping the symptoms will magically disappear—symptoms such as rectal bleeding, lingering abdominal pain, or chronic constipation. The stark reality is that the symptoms do not go away; they get worse. And medical attention for uninsured Americans usually comes too late.

The circumstances of my father's death in 1991 were a little bit different. While there was very little that might have been done to save my mother back in 1979, my father did not have to die of a stroke when he did.

My father could have been the poster child of the typical blue-collar male American. His way of showing love for his family was not by saying the words "I love you" all the time, hugging us all the time, or sitting down and having family meetings or playing board games. The only way he knew how to show that he cared for us was going out and working every day so that our mother could pay the rent and buy groceries. His hands were dirty every day as he worked putting in and taking out pipes, sewer lines, etc. He had a few drinks on the weekend and unfortunately sometimes during the week as well.

After our mother's death, he had to take over all the tasks she had handled—which was just about everything. It would be an understatement to say that he struggled with many issues for the first few years after my mother's death, but we managed to make it through. He understood the importance of education for his children but had no concept of what to do to help guide us in making the correct educational choices. All the decisions my sister and I made about going to college pretty much were made by talking to our guidance counselors, getting brochures, and then letting our father know what we were thinking about. There was not a whole lot he could bring to the process.

When I decided to go to Syracuse University, my father supported the decision. He went to Syracuse in 1982 to drop me off and he returned in 1986 to pick me up. That was the extent of his involvement in my college experience. The fact that he wasn't more involved with me when I was in college doesn't bother me. I knew who my father was, and I knew that he was very proud of me when I graduated from college and then became a second lieutenant in the United States Army.

In the late '80s, I took a job with Merck Pharmaceuticals and moved from Brooklyn down to South Carolina. Talk about culture shock! I moved from Brooklyn to Florence, the fifth largest city in the state of South Carolina. My sister stayed in New York until 1989, when she moved to Miami, Florida. My sister and I both got married in 1990. With his kids now gone, my father did what he had done all his life. He went to work. He came home. He had his drinks.

My uncle, who lived with my father at that time, told me that at some point my father started becoming very ill. He was feeling weak. He was having chest pains. He was having night sweats. Nevertheless, he did what he had always done, regardless of the circumstances. He went to work. It eventually got to the point that he was so weak and ill at work that his supervisor sent him home.

My father never went to the doctor. The only time that I know of my father ever going to a physician was when he had broken his leg about ten years earlier. Now that he was sick, he chose the position many people choose under similar circumstances. He chose to ignore the symptoms and hoped that they would go away. Soon his condition worsened while he was at home, and my uncle gave him the choice of either driving him to a nearby emergency room or calling an ambulance to get him—but either way he was going to the hospital that day. Reluctantly he went to the ER.

After a series of tests, he was immediately admitted to the hospital. His diagnosis was endocarditis, an infection of one of the valves of his heart. He had gone to the dentist a few weeks earlier for some tooth extractions, and after the dental work was done a bacterial vegetative growth developed in his heart that required immediate antibiotic intervention. My sister went to see him. I stayed down in Atlanta and did what I had always been accustomed to doing: I continued to go to work every day. I stayed in contact with my sister and my father by telephone.

During the initial phases of the antibiotic treatment, my father seemed to be getting better, and since the doctors said he was improving, my sister returned to Florida. A few days later, a repeat echocardiogram showed that the vegetative growth around his heart valve had actually gotten worse. The resident who was assigned to my father (I had no idea who the attending physician or internist was) informed my father and three of my uncles that my father had to have immediate valve replacement. The valve replacement did not take place in the hospital where my father was, and plans were immediately made to transfer him to another facility for the procedure.

My father and my uncles were concerned about the hospital he was going to be transferred to because it was the same hospital that my mother had died in several years earlier. In addition it did not enjoy a very good reputation in the community. One of my aunts was a nurse at New York University (NYU) hospital and tried to arrange to get my father there for the valve replacement. Unfortunately there were no beds available on that particular day at NYU hospital. He would have to wait in the hospital he was currently in for one more day.

That one-day delay turned out to be a death sentence. He had gotten up out of bed to go to the bathroom when a piece of the clot broke off from around the valve of his heart, floated up to his brain, and caused strokes in several areas. He never regained consciousness. He died a few days later at NYU hospital.

Who do you blame for what happened to my father? Do you blame my father for not being more aggressive about his condition and going to the doctor sooner? Do you blame the resident who took care of my father for not being more aggressive and letting my uncles know that if immediate surgery did not take place my father could die? Do you blame my uncles, who played a pivotal role in convincing my father to wait to get into a hospital bed at NYU? Should I blame myself for not taking time off from work to go to New York and be with my father the entire time he was hospitalized? Or do you just blame the system?

One thing I am sure of is that if my father and my uncles had been a little bit more educated about the seriousness of my father's illness, he would be alive today. Situations like my father's occur every day in America. Ordinary working-class Americans get sick, and because of fear or ignorance—or lack of insurance—they ignore their symptoms, just as my father did, and then eventually suffer the consequences.

Forty-seven million Americans, most of whom are working families and their small children[1], live each day with the fear of getting sick and suffering the consequences. The number of uninsured Americans is disgraceful. There is no greater threat today to America than *not* dealing with the issue of healthcare. The imploding American healthcare system is far more threatening to our future than the current war in Iraq.

Though more than 3,000 troops have died overseas protecting us here in America[2], 18,000 people die annually because they lack healthcare insurance. Studies have shown that the uninsured consistently have poorer prognoses, including death, when compared to insured Americans with similar illnesses.[3] The statement that the U.S. healthcare system is the best in the world is arguable, especially when that healthcare system excludes more than 15 percent of the population.[4] How can it be the best in the world when it has a below-average life expectancy and above-average infant fatality rate compared to other industrialized nations? How can it be the best in the world when it has an above-average medical error rate and spends a more significant portion of its economy on healthcare when compared to other major industrialized nations?

To understand the problems with the U.S. healthcare system, one has first to understand the players. In the upcoming chapters, I outline the major players in this drama of healthcare. We have to understand the players and know the reasons they make the decisions they do. Once we have that information, we are better prepared to find solid solutions to fix this crisis in America called healthcare.

## CHAPTER II
# THE MEDICAL STUDENT
## The Glorified First-Round Draft Pick

One of the proudest things parents can do is introduce their child to someone by saying "This is my son …" or "This is my daughter, the doctor." It has been my own personal experience that my friends or relatives introduce me to others as Dr. Bennett far more often than I myself use the title. Everyone wants a doctor in the family.

When we ask kids in elementary school what they want to be when they grow up, more times than not one of the choices is "a doctor." As kids get older and start to separate themselves from the pack academically, the thought of one day becoming a doctor begins the slight push toward the profession—first by their family members and then themselves.

The first real test on the road to becoming a physician occurs in the last few years of high school. This is the first round of separation. The students that accelerate in math and science find themselves separating themselves from the doctor wannabes. The next big test comes at the college level. Every liberal arts institution fills with an incoming class of doctor wannabes.

Most of the freshman class makes it through the initial courses on their road to medicine—your biology, your chemistry, and calculus. Unfortunately in this first year quite a few candidates are lost to the college experience. They get caught up in the freedom of being away from home, being able to party all night, drinking alcohol, and being attracted to the opposite sex. They lose their academic focus. They end their first year with a 2.8 or 2.7 GPA, which essentially ends their dreams of becoming a physician.

There is virtually no recovery from a bad freshman year academically if one wishes to become a physician. That is the reality of the situation. Can you imagine that the competition for medical school is so intense that two mediocre semesters out of eight technically puts one out of the running? It's even worse in Canada, where anything short of a 3.75 GPA essentially ends your medical school dreams.[5]

The next major point of separation is sophomore year, with organic chemistry. The course is worth more credits than any other course you take in college. This course has traditionally separated the wheat from the chaff. I remember how terrified I was in my sophomore year when it came to organic chemistry, but I knew that if I did well in that course, I was well on my way toward finishing college with a legitimate opportunity to go to medical school.

After organic chemistry, with a little hard work, during the last two years, it's usually quite reasonable to raise a GPA into the 3.5 range and then apply for medical school. The next hurdle to get over is the MCATs, the Medical College Aptitude Tests. Like the SATs for college, the standardization exam for medical school is the MCAT, which is supposed to level the playing field. Yeah, right.

As with the SATs, those individuals with the financial resources to take a proper MCAT review course have a significant advantage over the rest of the field. Also, as with the SATs, minority groups tend to have less financial resources and are at an immediate disadvantage. It should also be said that because there are so few African American and Latino physicians who can pass on the know how to successfully negotiate the entire process for preparation for medical school, from high school through college and then the MCATs, this further limits the number of minorities that eventually become strong candidates for medical school.

I essentially went semester to semester through high school and college trying to gather information as I went. There was really no one I could turn to for guidance. All my friends in high school took SAT prep on weekends, while I could not afford to. I depended on an SAT review book I picked up at the local bookstore. I had no real structure in my SAT or MCAT preparation. My scores on both reflected that lack of preparation. I could not break 1,000 on my SAT, but I ended my first two semesters at Syracuse University with a 3.4 GPA and earned a B and an A in my sophomore year in organic chemistry. Unless all students have the same tools to prepare for the major exams that determine their future, there can never be a level playing field.

Once the MCATs are completed (with average or above-average scores), there comes the application and then the interview process for medical schools. By the way, the MCATs and the application for medical school should take place during one's junior year of college—a fact I was told by my pre-med advisor in my senior year of college. I was late with everything and therefore would not be able to go to medical school after graduation.

I haven't done the research but would guess that individuals who do not begin college after high school or graduate school after college are less likely to continue their education as planned. One gets a new job or starts a family, and further educational plans are indefinitely put off or never pursued. A wife and six years later, I finally applied to medical school.

Just as college basketball and football players prepare themselves for the upcoming draft to the NBA or NFL, so do potential medical school candidates prepare themselves for acceptance into medical school. Once interviewing is over, the waiting begins. As a potential medical student, you wait for that glorious acceptance letter in the mail. As a professional ballplayer during the NBA or NFL draft, you sit in a crowded auditorium or at home with your family, waiting for your name to be called and to be invited to the show. As a premedical college student, you wait for your acceptance letter—the invitation to *your* show, medical school.

Just like those athletes who are drafted, accepted medical students rejoice, celebrate, and are celebrated. They are the academic equivalent to the poor man's professional athlete. There are hugs, kisses, tears, parties, receptions, cards, presents, and sometimes there is even money. You feel very good about yourself. You are now one of the elite students who started a college career as a pre-med student and actually achieved your goal of getting into medical school. You are just four years away from obtaining one of the most coveted educational degrees, the MD (medical doctorate). Words cannot describe how happy and proud I felt when I was accepted to Morehouse School of Medicine. Finally, six years after college, I made it to the show.

Soon orientation begins at medical school. You meet and greet your classmates, sizing up the competition. Everyone believes that he or she is the smartest one in the bunch. During the first days of orientation, just as in college, you gravitate toward a core of individuals you believe are going to be your friends and your study partners in the upcoming years.

Then it hits: the first day of classes. Your biochemistry and your histology professors start from one corner of the blackboard and stop at the end of the other corner of the blackboard, across the room, or they blow through countless numbers of PowerPoint slides. Welcome to training camp. When the first day ends, all the confidence, all the arrogance, all the bravado disappears. Forget about being the smartest; you just want to survive. You can be cut in professional training camp if you do not make the grade and you can be cut in medical school if you do not make the grade.

I knew going into medical school that there were many students probably smarter than I was. I knew I would have to work harder than most to survive. I felt like Rudy (from the film of same name). After the first day of classes, you didn't just feel like you had a headache; you felt as if your brain was swelling from the volumes of information you had absorbed during that first day. The next day, the next week, and the next month didn't get any easier. I probably spent more time studying during my first two months of medical school than during my first two years of college.

For your first two years of medical school, there is no time to do anything but attend class, eat, study, and sleep when you can. However, it didn't matter how much time you studied during the week, exam times always meant countless all-nighters. In the first two years of medical school, reality hits: all the students you thought were smarter than you are taking the same examinations. There is no grading curve like in college. You can no longer count on those slouches you had in college that moved the bell curve in your favor. In medical school everyone is smart. Everyone is dedicated. Everyone is committed. Everyone can play ball.

Medical school is actually tougher on individuals who have families. When I attended medical school, I was married and soon had a little girl. All the hours in class—the labs, the study time, and the all-nighters—definitely puts a strain on one's marriage. The divorce rate for married medical students is right around 50 percent. That statistic proved to be true for my class. As the first two years go by, you become more accustomed to proper study discipline. The swelling in your brain starts subside.

After the first two years of medical school, which encompass the basic science or foundational medical knowledge, one encounters the first *major* medical exam—the United States Medical Licensure Examination, or Step 1 exam. This is the first of three major medical examinations that you have to take in order to be a licensed practitioner of medicine in the United States. Many medical schools do not allow students to continue into the clinical years of medicine until they have successfully passed this examination.

The USMLE – Step 1 examination is considered one of the most difficult licensure examinations in any profession. I remember taking two solid months, eight to ten hours a day, in steady preparation for that examination. I remember telling my wife that unless the house was on fire or someone was on the verge of death, not to bother me. I then locked myself in our bonus room and studied.

Once you pass the examination, you begin to "rotate" through what we call core clinical areas. Core clinicals include family practice, internal medicine, OB-GYN, psychiatry, pediatrics, and surgery. Everyone has a general idea what area of medicine he or she wishes to practice. When one has completed core rotations, one's experience during a particular rotation either confirms the specialty one wishes to go into, or after the exposure to other areas of medicine, one changes one's mind.

While during the basic science years it was okay to be shy and reserved, devoting yourself to study, not making yourself known, the clinical takes on a new perspective. In clinicals, in order to shine, you have to show your attending physician that you are a very motivated individual. You have to prepare yourself for rounds in the morning and be ready with the answer to any question that the attending might ask. You have to be willing to come early and stay late. You have to show that you can bounce back after criticism. You become mired elbow deep in what is termed "scut" work. Scut work is essentially all the things that attending physicians, residents, nurses, and everyone else involved with the patient chooses to not do.

Usually there are four to five medical students rotating together on any particular core rotation. If there is an opportunity to do a particular procedure, you elbow your colleagues out of the way to get to the front of the line to perform the procedure, making sure your attending or your resident sees how aggressive you are. Whether you enjoy a particular specialty or not, for the two or three months you spend on that rotation, you had better show a positive attitude or risk getting a poor evaluation. If you are completing a rotation in the core specialty of which you plan to make a career, you had better make your best effort to impress your attending physicians in order to get a glowing evaluation and letter of recommendation.

Your clinical medicine years are when you get an initial taste of what patient-physician interaction is like. Most teaching hospitals that have residents or medical students have a high number of indigent or poor patients—patients who look up to anyone they believe can help them, even the lowly medical student in the short white coat. I remember many days and nights staying by patients' bedsides to answer questions to help them make a difficult decision regarding their care or to provide emotional support before they underwent a procedure. In many cases the medical student probably spends more time with a particular patient than either the resident or the attending physician.

One of the things that hits you in the stomach during these clinical years is your introduction to death. You see many patients. Some have positive outcomes and some have negative outcomes. What becomes very evident from the very beginning is the ability for nurses, residents, and attending physicians to move on after a patient has died. To say they are indifferent to death would not be accurate, but admittedly there is not a whole lot of time spent reflecting on a life that is no longer with us.

This was brought home to me when on the first day of my clinical rotation in internal medicine I was assigned to a terminal patient who had pneumonia. He was an elderly man. When I walked into the room, he was unconscious. I spoke to him, but he wasn't responsive. I noticed that his IV had stopped dripping, so I attempted to adjust the IV site in his arm. While I adjusted the line, he started bleeding suddenly from the IV site. I remember feeling very panicked internally, thinking that I had done something wrong. I continued the adjustment, the IV drip started, I was able to stop the bleeding, and I taped the IV line back in place on his arm.

The next morning I arrived a little bit early to go check on my patient. I walked into an empty room—no patient, the bed perfectly made, the room spotless. Alarmed, I ran to my resident and asked what happened to "Mr. Smith." The resident responded, "Oh, he passed away during the night. By the way, here is a new patient. Go work him up before rounds." That was it. That was the extent of the discussion. Mr. Smith had passed away and I was just assigned another patient to follow.

I spent the next few days wondering if I had done something wrong with his IV line. Maybe during my adjustment had air gotten into the line or some bubbles had gotten into the IV site; that really was not likely. More than likely Mr. Smith succumbed to his pneumonia. I do not remember anyone at the resident or attending level actually spending any time with me discussing the passing of my patient; that would have been nice and I'd have welcomed and appreciated it.

After two years of witnessing patients die—in the emergency room, after surgery, during surgery, during internal medicine, during OB-GYN, during pediatrics—I too found myself becoming a little bit indifferent to the process of death. Please do not misunderstand me. While the patient is alive, everyone is working feverishly to do everything possible to save a life. Nevertheless, once the patient dies, everyone moves on.

As medical students we are so caught up in trying to impress our attendings that we begin to lose sight of the people we are actually trying to help. I remember vividly one such example. One task that medical students are usually assigned is completing a history and physical examination of a particular patient. The history records the patient's chief complaint; the symptoms of that complaint; any past medical problems; any past surgeries; allergies; social history including alcohol abuse or use, tobacco use, or illicit drug use; the profession of the particular patient; marital status; and any significant family history that may contribute to the patient's situation. We also do a review during which we ask questions from head to toe about symptoms such as headache, chest pain, shortness of breath, nausea, etc.

For most of the core rotation, taking a history is quite easy since the patient comes to the hospital and is lying in the emergency room bed and you can stand there and get the information needed from the patient or from any family member who may be present. Getting that information becomes extremely difficult during a time of trauma. I remember when I was doing my surgical rotation. We were down in the emergency room and a trauma came in. A young man, about eighteen years old, had been shot in the abdomen.

Being a part of the trauma team, we were doing what we normally do, trying to stabilize the patient as best as possible. Another medical student and I initially attempted to get a history from the patient. That soon proved to be impossible because our patient was sedated and was slipping in and out of consciousness. The medical student that was with me directed her questions to the patient's aunt, who was standing next to him in the trauma bay.

The medical student initially started to ask relevant questions: where was he when he was shot, what happened, did he have any particular medical conditions that we needed to be aware of, was he taking any medications, was he allergic to anything. Quite understandably, the aunt was very distracted as she was trying to see what was going on with her nephew. She did her best, though, to answer the medical student's questions.

After getting what we considered pertinent information, the medical student did not stop. She continued on and on asking irrelevant after irrelevant question. I could see the aunt's face, and it was obvious she was getting quite annoyed with the student. I remember walking over to the student and saying, "That's enough. I think we got what we need." The student arrogantly responded by saying, "I've got to get my history done." She clearly could not have cared less about the emotional state of the aunt or the patient lying on the gurney in front of her. Her only objective was to obtain as much information as she could at that time to complete her paperwork. I understand that that student eventually ended up going into pediatrics, unbelievably.

Your clinical years are also when you are introduced to the "on call" concept. Every two, three, four, or five days, depending on the rotation, you spend a night at the hospital, waiting for your pager to go off in the middle of the night, then meeting your resident in the pertinent department. On a good night, you would be awakened only once or twice. On a bad night, you never made it back to your call room.

Long hours in the hospital, call, competing with your fellow medical students, kissing the butt of your resident or your attendings, and doing all the scut work assigned to you is, for the most part, your life for the last two years of medical school. When it is all said and done, you spent your first two years with your nose in a book, taking exam, after exam, after exam. You spent your last two years going to the hospital in the morning and coming back home at night. You had no clue about anything that was going on in your community, in your state, in your country, around the world. Maybe you remembered who was president of the United States, but only if no one new was elected during the four years you were in medical school.

Now it is almost over. You have picked your specialty; you graduate with your MD degree. You think your life has now improved because you are no longer a medical student. You are now a resident and the scut work belongs to someone else. You really believe that your life will be better as a resident. Oh, what a major mental mistake you have just made. I always wondered, as a medical student, why residents had such a poor attitude and a permanent pissed-off look on their faces. I was about to find out myself, as a PGY1, postgraduate year-one intern; the first year of residency.

# CHAPTER III
# INTERNSHIP
## A Living Hell

There is a saying, "No man is an island," but as an intern, one seems to be stranded on an island by oneself an awful lot. As a medical student, it was virtually impossible to *really* mess up anything since there were so many people above you. You have an intern above you, that intern had a senior resident, and that senior resident had an attending. I found that when I was an intern the general understanding from my senior residents was that I was to handle my business without bothering them unless I absolutely had to. "Absolutely" meant someone was about to die. You also did not want to call your upper level too often or word would start spreading throughout the program that you were an incompetent intern.

Instead of calling on my upper levels when I was in a pinch, such as when a patient had shortness of breath or chest pain, I went to the patient's bedside. I spoke with the patient, I looked through the chart, the medication list, the patient's history, the labs, the notes of the previous physical, and then I did my own physical. If I still couldn't figure out what was wrong, I pulled out one of the several books I kept in my pockets. I only had one mission; I only had one goal: stabilize the patient and make sure they live until morning and the cavalry arrived. Only if my patient was about to go into cardiac arrest would I call my upper level.

As an intern there was one physical state you always were in: sleep deprivation. There were times when I drove home after I had finished call and didn't remember how I actually made my way home. Other times I remember driving off the road, onto the curb and back onto the road again, the jolt startling me back to awareness. Work as an intern wasn't like a regular job where you just put in long, tough hours. There were constant times of adrenaline rushes, bouts of depression, bouts of anxiety, and severe mood swings all in a single day. I remember times of being both physically and emotionally exhausted. At two or three o'clock in the morning, my pager would go off and I would have to go back to the hospital. I would always try my best not to show the patient my frustration or let them believe it was their fault that they were having problems at two or three o'clock in the morning.

Unfortunately sometimes one just couldn't help it. It made it much harder and sometimes almost unbearable when I found myself taking care of problems that should have been handled by the previous medical team—the team that was in the hospital prior to 5:00 p.m. There were days that you started call at five o'clock and ten minutes later you would get a call from the emergency room to tell you that there were four or five patients waiting to be admitted—patients that should and could have been admitted and worked up prior to five o'clock. You would get down to the emergency room and find patients all over the place and you were on your own. The ER doctors were there, but they already had their hands full. You'd walk over to the first gurney and start the process: history, physical examination, labs, tests, and admission orders. If something is happening to someone on the floor, you get the call.

As a family practice intern, you are the only physician on the floor. If there is a code in the emergency room, you get the call to go down and assist the ER doctor in the code. If there is a problem in the ICU, you get the call. If a patient comes in to Labor and Delivery, once again, you get the call. If a general surgeon has to come to the hospital in the middle of the night to perform a procedure or a GYN has to come in to perform a procedure, as usual, you get the call to assist. Call can sometimes be a living hell. Remember, in June you were a fourth-year medical student with few worries and responsibilities. In July you are an intern thrown into the fire. Your decisions may determine whether someone lives or dies.

You successfully survived your intern year, but the celebration is short-lived. You are about to become a PGY2, postgraduate year-two resident. As a PGY2 in family medicine or internal medicine, you are the catchall person. You are not only responsible for all the things that you do yourself, but you must catch all the mistakes that the interns make. You have more call and more responsibilities, including teaching interns and medical students. If you are an intern and are on call and push comes to shove, you can always wake up your second- or third-year resident and have them come help you in the hospital. However, as a second-year resident, there is no backup in the hospital. If you need help, you have to call the third-year resident or the attending at their home and ask them to come in to help you. That call is not one you want to make too often.

As a PGY2 you know just enough to be dangerous if you decide to become too aggressive in patient care. At this time you *must* know what you *do not* know, and call for help. By now you should have successfully completed your United States Medical Licensure Exams, steps one, two, and three. After successful completion of step three, you are eligible for medical licensure. By the time you became a PGY2, you would have passed all the medical exams needed to be a licensed physician in any state of the country. You should be a reasonably competent physician.

If one chooses to leave residency and go into private practice, one can legally do so. Leaving residency before completion is not a good idea, though, since most hospitals require that one complete residency to become eligible for their medical staff. Another good reason not to leave residency early is that one would not be eligible for board certification in any specialty if one had not completed a postgraduate program.

One thing that can be said about your second and third years of residency is that you see a multitude of things that become indelibly etched into your mind. It becomes quite clear that people who are uninsured and/ or indigent and/or mentally challenged are the ones medical students and residents prod, stick and poke, twist and bend, with respect, all as part of the medical educational process. Medical students and residents can poke and stick because every teaching hospital requires patients to sign a release form indicating that the hospital is a teaching facility and as such not only attending physicians but also residents and/or medical students may see these patients.

Most teaching hospitals have a high census of uninsured or indigent patients who essentially volunteer, perhaps unwillingly, for resident and medical student training. I say *unwillingly* because what choice do you have if you are uninsured? You have to go where someone will see you, and that's usually not the upscale private hospital in town.

Residents and students practice putting a central line in patients' necks. Sometimes they accidentally miss the vein and stick the needle in the artery; you know you missed and hit an artery when blood spews across the room. They practice putting a central line in the subclavian vein that runs above the lung. You know you missed the vein when you accidentally puncture the lung, putting air in the chest cavity, causing what is termed a pneumothorax. They practice putting central lines into the femoral vein in the upper medial thigh, sometimes missing the vein and plunging the needle into the femoral nerve, causing a severe electric shock to shoot through the patient's lower extremities. When a patient is unconscious and stops breathing, they practice putting in an intubation tube down the patient's throat to help them to breathe, but unfortunately they sometimes miss the pharynx and end up introducing the tube into the esophagus. All of this said, every effort is always made to get the procedure right the first time and alleviate as much suffering as possible for the patients.

These procedural complications are not unique to medical students or residents; senior doctors sometimes have those complications as well. When a student or a young resident attempts an unfamiliar procedure, there is always proper supervision—supervision that can, if necessary, jump in at any time and limit the risk of permanent injury to the patient. For the next generation of medical providers to be properly trained, they have to cut their teeth with real patients. This is why I believe America has to be more sensitive to patients who agree to participate in the process of teaching medical students and residents. If I had to be admitted for a routine issue, I would choose a private, non-teaching facility. I would prefer that my wife deliver our children without four medical students, two residents, and one attending in the room. Because I am insured, I have that choice.

Nonetheless, teaching hospitals usually have the best trained and most up-to-date physicians in their areas—physicians that are constantly reading and learning, and writing the literature for their particular specialty. Almost all prominent cancer or trauma facilities are teaching hospitals. If one is admitted to a teaching hospital, that may also mean that several doctors are responsible for one's care. Usually, with coordination, the more physicians that are taking care of you, the least likely it is that something will fall through the cracks. That concept again definitely works best when there is one point physician responsible for your overall care. That usually is the attending primary care or internist physician and his or her team.

Teaching hospitals, as opposed to smaller community hospitals, always have in-house physicians to handle emergencies. The latest technologies and the most recently available experimental drugs are usually tested at teaching institutions. If I were critically injured, a teaching facility would be my first choice for treatment.

# CHAPTER IV
# MEDICAL RESIDENCY
## Tragic Memories for a Lifetime

A significant number of the patients residents take care of are the ones frequently overlooked by society. These include the poor, the elderly, the mentally challenged, and the homeless.[6] Many residency training hospitals are in poor neighborhoods where the availability of other medical resources is limited.[7] I remember several times getting to the hospital in the wee hours of the morning and seeing several homeless people stumbling about outside under the awnings of the hospital, trying to keep warm.

When it gets too cold, usually those over forty go into the emergency room complaining of chest pain or shortness of breath. They know that a complaint of chest pain gets them an immediate ticket out of the cold. They also know what to say to lead a physician toward diagnosing a cardiac problem rather than something else. They are well aware that a cardiac diagnosis gives them a warm place to stay and three meals a day for at least twenty-four hours. Some people really know how to work the system.

There was an incident once when I was working in the asthma room at my teaching hospital. A woman came in with four to five shopping bags and two children who appeared to be her grandchildren. She had called an ambulance, saying that she was having an asthma attack and had to be taken by ambulance to the emergency room. When she got there, she was quickly worked up and was given an Albuterol breathing treatment. Asthmatic patients who have a lot of trouble breathing do not commonly show dramatic improvement after only one treatment, but this particular lady perked up quite quickly after her one treatment.

She picked up her bags and was about to walk out of the asthma room when I said to her, "You recovered pretty quickly from your asthma attack, didn't you?" Her response was, "I didn't have a ride to get downtown, but I knew if I had an asthma attack I could call an ambulance that would bring me down here, and I needed to go shopping." She then turned, picked up her bags and walked out of the asthma room with her grandchildren. Taxpayers' money financed her excursion.

All teaching hospitals also have their share of alcoholics who end up in the hospital suffering from delirium tremors and requiring full admission. Every teaching hospital has it share of diabetics in full-blown diabetic ketoacidosis, which if not treated could result in death. Some of the same individuals end up in this situation monthly because they do not take their medication as instructed. We used to call them frequent flyers.

There is also the severe-diabetic foot-ulcer patient. This is a diabetic individual who usually does not take their medication regularly for several "reasons." They say they didn't have the money to refill prescriptions. They were "in denial" about their disease process. They were taking their medication incorrectly. They were afraid or intimidated by the healthcare process and didn't know how to seek help.

Whatever the case, their diabetes gets out of control. They get a cut on their foot. The cut begins to turn into a sore. You would think at this point they would seek medical attention, but you would be wrong. They believe the infection will get better without interference. It doesn't. The sore gets much worse. The infection eats away at the toes of the foot. They don't feel any pain or discomfort, because their diabetic state is such that the nerve endings in their foot have become completely dysfunctional.

As their foot begins to rot, the patient becomes used to the odor generated. If they live alone, there is no one else who might notice this strong odor. The time comes when more than one digit is gone and the foot is now almost completely black, and they finally turn up in the emergency room. The odor of a diabetic foot infection is something that never leaves you, or your clothes, your skin, or hair. The patient goes to surgery and ends up losing the infected foot. In reality, they end up losing their entire lower leg—the infamous BKA, or below-the-knee amputation. Diabetes is the number-one cause of lower-limb amputation not related to trauma, the number-one cause of acquired blindness, and the number-one cause of kidney failure leading to dialysis in the United States.[8]

Another type of patient who is more than likely encountered in residency in primary care is a pregnant drug addict, someone who cares more about getting a hit from crack cocaine than taking care of her unborn child. I remember a middle-of-the-night summons for an emergency delivery. When I got to Labor and Delivery, I saw in one of the beds a morbidly obese woman; she was in and out of consciousness because of the effects of some drugs she had just used. She was somewhere between four and five months pregnant, had not had any prenatal care, and now was about to abort the fetus.

I had to have two nurses' help; one holding back one leg, while the other held back the other leg. All of us did out best to tell the patient, when she was conscious, to push, but she was not making much of an effort. To complicate matters even more, it was a breach delivery. The leg delivered first, then the arms and the upper torso. I had to go in to ensure that the head came attached to the body. When it was over, I held in my hand a tiny infant who struggled for every breath. The neonatal team came from the teaching hospital a few miles away. I don't know what became of that baby, but I was didn't believe his survival was possible.

After delivering the placenta and then starting to clean up the mother, I asked myself what could possibly have happened in her life to bring her to such a point. What tragic circumstance would cause a person to harm herself by using crack cocaine or other drugs and then knowingly use those drug during pregnancy, blinding herself to the effects it would have on her child? The mother and baby were transferred to another facility, and I don't know what became of her. I can only hope that she eventually got her life in order.

One thing that I never became good at as a resident was informing a family that a loved one had passed away. Our clinical psychology attending taught us that when relating sad news to a patient's family we should gather them all together in a private room, make sure we sit down with them, and only then tell them the bad news. Sitting down with them puts everyone on an equal level. The physician should not stand over the family as if in a position of superiority. We were told not to use phrases like "passed away" and "is no longer with us" but to rather say "Everyone did all they could, but it wasn't enough" and to follow with "Your love one has died," thus leaving no room for misinterpretation.

There are always certain patients you took care of that you knew were going to die within a few days. You would enter the ICU and see the family around the bed. They would look so optimistic, clinging to the slightest hope that you could possibly give them. I always told patients' families the truth, but I was always very careful not to take away all hope. I firmly believe that everyone needs a little hope, all the way to the very end. I can still see the faces of some of the families when I told them it was highly unlikely that their loved one would recover and they needed to make whatever arrangements they thought necessary. I could see how crushed and how devastated they were.

It is one thing breaking the news to a family whose loved one was critically ill and may live a few days before eventually dying. That allows the family to prepare for the outcome. It is a completely different situation when an individual is involved in a car accident, stabbing, or shooting and they do not make it out of the trauma bay. Then you have to go out to tell the family that they have died. After breaking the news, you have to sit there for a few minutes and watch them just fall apart. You can't cry with them. You aren't supposed to. You kindly say, "I am Dr. Bennett. If there is anything more I can do, please let me know." You give a hug to those who need it, and then you walk away and leave them to deal with their grief.

I have never personally cried over the death of any particular patient. I have been sad, depressed, and sympathetic, but I have never cried, because I was conditioned to not cry. You cannot cry in front of your patient or their family; it makes you look weak, or so I've been told.

There was, however, one occasion during my residency when I almost broke down. This case also involved Labor and Delivery. I was on call one Christmas week when one of the OB-GYNs at the community hospital asked me to assist him on a delivery. He said that there was no hurry, that I could take my time. He was going to have to induce the mother. The baby was due in four days, but the mother came into the OB-GYN's office stating that she had not felt the baby move for an extended period.

The OB-GYN had to inform this family, this mother- and father-to-be, that their baby had died in the womb four days before delivery. From the ultrasound it looked as if—as the baby was positioning itself to come down the birth canal—the umbilical cord had become wrapped around his neck as he descended and he had strangled. To make circumstances more tragic, this same young couple had lost a two- or three-year-old child to a car accident years earlier. They had one living child.

So, during the week of Christmas, I went in to help this attending physician deliver this full-term dead baby. When the baby delivered, as the ultrasound had indicated, the umbilical cord was wrapped tightly around the baby's neck three or four times. Once the baby was delivered, I wrapped him up and placed him in his mother's arms. I stood there and watched mother, father, and grandmother cry, and yet even after undergoing that ordeal, they managed to say, "God is good." They named the baby Jeremiah, after the prophet in the Bible. Let me remind you again that all this happened the week of Christmas. What would Christmas mean for this family in years to come? All they would think about would be little Jeremiah.

These are just some of the events that take a mental toll on young medical residents. There is a physical price to pay as a resident as well: constant fatigue, anxiety, depression, weight loss and weight gain, horrible diets, eating at ridiculous times of the day, exposure to tuberculosis, and exposure to AIDS. I feel that one year of residency will take two years off my life. Residency took an emotional toll as well as a physical toll on me personally. I developed migraine headaches while in residency. I got shingles during my surgical rotation in residency. I got stuck by needles in the trauma bay from patients and didn't know their HIV status; that was a very trying time of my life.

I was in the trauma bay trying to draw blood from a patient who was thrashing around in pain. He made a violent movement, and the needle jumped from his arm to my finger. I felt a slight pinch but hoped that the needle had not actually gone through my rubber gloves into my finger. Slowly I saw blood begin to accumulate underneath my glove and realized I had been stuck. I didn't tell anybody. Sometime later I developed shingles. I asked some of the infectious-disease doctors what the possible causes of shingles were in a thirty-five-year-old male. The response was HIV. I looked in all my textbooks, and they all confirmed what the infectious-disease doctors were telling me: that the most common cause of shingles in a thirty-five-year-old male was HIV.

I went to the clinic to be tested. Those were the three longest days of my life. I remember not telling my wife. I did not want to alarm her unnecessarily. For three days I thought about my life. I thought about everyone in my life. I thought about my past. I thought about my family's future without me. I thought my wife would lose her husband and my children, aged four and two, would lose their father. I probably thought about the same things my mother thought about when she knew she was dying and would leave behind a spouse and young children. If I did turn out to be HIV positive, I thought about people talking behind my back. I thought about the looks of pity I would get from friends. I thought about other residents being relieved that it had happened to me and not them. I tried to barter with God to spare me. Needless to say, I did not sleep for three days.

Then I received the results: my test was negative; I was *not* HIV positive. I had my life back. I could finally exhale. The air smelled crisp. The sun seemed brighter. For some reason God chose to spare me. But for the three days before I got the good news, I realized that no matter what else was going on in one's life—no matter the financial stress, the family relationship stress—nothing else mattered if you or a loved one became critically ill. Nothing matters if you have a terminal disease.

At least I had health insurance and could have gotten proper treatment if I had turned out to be HIV positive. Those treatments could have probably have extended my life. However, what about the uninsured individuals who contract HIV? One can imagine the double tragedy they endure: first the devastating diagnosis and second the lack of health insurance to extend or save their life.

These have been only a few of the stories of life as a medical resident. After being physically and emotionally beaten up for four years of medical school, then three years of residency, it was time to enter life as a practicing physician. Things would *have* to get better, one would think!

# CHAPTER V

# THE PRACTICING PHYSICIAN
## McFly Becomes the Point Guard

It is time to get back to George McFly and examine how "Dr. McFly" came to be. After the average practicing physician spends a minimum of seven to nine years of study and preparation for medical school and their specialty, they emerge from the tunnel and back into society.

New physicians find doors opening for them left and right. They are now in a position to earn a substantial amount of money. Everyone seems to want their attention—from financial planners to homebuilders, to hospitals, to charities. Unfortunately the average physician has had very little business preparation during the seven to nine years of medical school and residency, so what typical new physicians do is natural. They seek advice from senior physicians. Senior clinicians, months earlier, were their attending physicians and were greatly respected and admired.

New physicians feel obligated to continue to listen to the conservative and safe advice of their senior peers. This may be one reason physicians continue to be one of the most conservative groups in the country from generation to generation. I remember a speech at a financial seminar more than twenty years ago where a speaker said, "When a physicians decides to put their money in an investment, that's the time to pull your money out because all the profit has already been made." When it comes time for any type of business investment, physicians analyze everything and still cannot make a decision.

Another place new physicians turn to for advice is their local hospital administration. This is like a well-fed mouse asking a starving cat for advice. Here is a news flash: for-profit hospitals are in business for one reason: for profit. The advice and direction a hospital administration gives a new physician will always be in the hospital's benefit. Hospital administrators are a new physician's best friend until the physician crosses them. When that happens the cat puts on his bib and it's time to eat.

Depending how nice we want to be, the typical U.S. physician is either a reluctant warrior or intimidated sheep. These are the amazing facts, though: of the two trillion spent annually in the United States on healthcare, physicians are the ones who write the prescriptions, write the orders, admit the patients, keep patients in the hospital, and pretty much dictate where all that money is spent—yet, like the sheep we are, we have little say in setting the agenda or the direction of healthcare in the future. Instead we delegate all our authority to the insurance companies, to government, to the lawyers, to hospitals and to the pharmaceutical companies. Physicians in America are completely emasculated. How did we get to this point?

Remember again that we are dealing with individuals who have had their noses firmly planted in textbooks since the ninth grade: studying hard in high school to get good grades for college, studying hard in college to get good grades for medical school, studying hard in medical school to get to a good residency program, then surviving that residency program. All that we concentrated on for almost ten years was medicine and our patients. There was no time for business. There was no time for financial planning. There was no time for politics.

Doctors are good at what we do because of the thousands of hours of preparation we put into doing exactly what we now do, patient care. When I attend continuing medical education (CME) conferences, the majority of our time, even during breaks, is spent talking about patients and improving patient outcomes, not about the business of medicine.

I did not go to medical school right after college; instead I went to work for Merck, Sharp and Dohme as a pharmaceutical representative in Florence, South Carolina. I enjoyed my life as a representative, talking to doctors about drugs. This was back in the mid to late 1980s, and respect for physicians was still there.

I say things have changed because I remember a particular situation surrounding the prescription nicotine patch for smokers, Habitrol. In 1990 I changed companies and was working for Geigy Pharmaceuticals in Atlanta, Georgia. Habitrol was one of my products. Habitrol is a nicotine patch that helps people stop smoking. Something was about to happen in the pharmaceutical industry—something that had never happened before. Geigy was actually going to get the go-ahead from the Food and Drug Administration to advertise a prescription drug on television. I remember how excited we were as representatives that one of the drugs we were promoting was going to be on television.

The corporate hierarchy at Geigy made two things clear: first, we were going to be spending about twenty million dollars on advertising, and second, the commercial was going to be carefully crafted in an effort to not put physicians on the spot or upset the FDA. Geigy actually feared a backlash from physicians if patients saw the commercial and went to a doctor's office demanding Habitrol. Because the pharmaceutical industry heavily depended upon the doctor-rep relationship to get their drugs prescribed and access to physicians was already limited, upsetting doctors would not be a good idea for any company.

Let me digress a moment and discuss the pharmaceutical rep-doctor relationship. I was taught in residency not to trust pharmaceutical reps; we were told "they are salesmen who care only about peddling their product. Get all the pens, pads, and lunches you can, but don't listen to them." Naturally I took exception to that position, considering I was one of those sales representatives for five years before starting medical school. Anyway, back to Habitrol.

Even though Geigy was cautious regarding the content of the commercial, by the time it aired the FDA had cut 50 percent out of the original version. The FDA at that time stood strongly against compromising standards in favor of the pharmaceutical industry. It can now be argued that the pendulum has swung to the other side, considering recent FDA decisions in favor of the pharmaceutical industry. There have been complaints that the FDA has approved new drugs for market too soon before drugs are adequately tested. What else could one expect, considering the lobby strength of the juggernaut drug industry?

If I remember correctly, the FDA did not want much detailed prescribing information in the Habitrol commercial. Much of the prescribing information that the FDA cut back then now appears in every drug commercial you see on television today. Lobby, lobby, lobby!

In time, and with pressure on the FDA, pharmaceutical companies realized that a far greater drug marketing tool than the rep-physician relationship was a new tactic called "the informed patient." It was far more effective to have patients go into a physician's office and demand a particular product than to have a rep detail the product to the physician. Who cares if they ticked off the physician? They realized that if patients ask for a particular drug, a doctor was more likely to prescribe it.

If a patient complains about having erectile dysfunction, ED, I first try to correct the underlying possible causes, such as uncontrolled hypertension or diabetes. Once proper therapeutic intervention is made in that arena, I would initiate treatment for the erectile dysfunction with one of the approved drugs. Two things have happened in recent years. First, patients come in, immediately want a pill for ED, and *do not care* about first correcting the underlying cause. Second, patients tell me what pill they want, based on the ad they saw on television. When reps detail drugs to me, they are on the spot to convince me to prescribe their products. Because of the preponderance of drug advertising directed to the public, patients put *me* on the hot seat to try to make them understand why they should not be on a product they saw on TV or in the paper—or a in magazine, on a blimp, or on a billboard.

So the gamble has paid off in spades for the pharmaceutical industry. Under the cloak of "informing the public," what the pharmaceutical industry has achieved is the ability to force the hand of physicians. Of course, the industry always protects itself by saying "Talk to your doctor about it." With time constraints being what they are already for physicians and patient encounters, spending more time explaining to a patient why something they saw on television may be inappropriate for their particular situation is burdensome.

Some patients get more demanding and try to convince you that they are right by repeating what they heard in the commercial. "No the commercial says this, and the commercial says that." Others, when you explain why the drug is inappropriate to their particular condition, look at you with a very strange look on their faces, as if they are debating whether you are incompetent and whether or not to trust you and believe what you're telling them.

Drug commercials do not inform the public; they undermine physicians. Moreover, they do exactly what the pharmaceutical industry intended: they drive sales. Many physicians, myself included, because of undue patient pressure, occasionally give in and prescribe drugs that are overpriced.

A classic example of this is drugs used for acid reflux. The over-the-counter proton pump inhibitor Prilosec is indicated for gastric reflux disease. Yet physicians still prescribe more expensive prescription proton pump inhibitors, such as Nexium, the purple pill for acid reflux. Some doctors prescribe the medication because the patient saw it on television and they thought it would work for them. Some doctors prescribe it because the pharmaceutical rep that markets prescription proton pump inhibitors constantly pushes the product. Physicians here again are at the frontline, but when push comes to shove, we give in.

Physicians fight other battles. As much as we would love to spend more time counseling our patients, we can't. We have to double-book because of patient cancellations or no-shows. We double-book to ensure we see enough patients to meet our monthly overhead. Of course, you always risk having those days when everyone shows up, leading to quite a stressful situation for the patient, for the physician's staff, and for the physician. Medicine has become a business, and like it or not, physicians have to see greater volumes of patients to stay in business.

In the primary-care setting, the physician needs to see a minimum of twenty-five patients per day to be profitable. Physicians in a primary-care/family-practice setting have the highest overhead of any other specialty and the lowest reimbursement of any other specialty.[9] Quite a combination. That is why we need to see a certain volume of patients on a daily basis. Our reimbursement is low because the insurance industry dictates to us how much they will pay, when they are willing pay, or if they will pay.[10]

The average physician does not have the time or the business savvy to negotiate reasonable deals with insurance companies, and we take what they give us, equitable or not. To make things worse for those physicians who actually try to stand up to the insurance industry by not accepting a certain rate, the physician next door will gladly accept the lower rates in order to capture more patients. It is like crabs in a barrel, each one trying to climb to the top.

Every physician has horror stories about billing. Actually the horror stories aren't about billing. The horror stories are about collecting your money after you've seen a patient. Insurance companies find every possible conceivable reason not to pay physicians, or not to pay us in a timely manner, or pay us less. They inundate you with volumes of paperwork, rule changes, procedure changes, and modifications. They do that because they know the average physician will allow them to get away with it.

We collect forty cents on every dollar we bill. Correction: the insurance companies agree to pay us forty cents for every dollar we bill. At the end of any given year, 10 percent of collectible dollars are written off because of lack of payment. Therefore, we probably average a payment of thirty-six cents for every dollar we bill. Can any industry run a successful business collecting 36 percent of their receivables? Physicians are thus forced to overbook, and we see as many patients as we can because we know there is a strong likelihood we will not be collecting any money from one out of ten patients of the patients we see. As a patient, if you want your doctor to spend more time with you, tell your insurance provider to pay his or her invoices.

Next on the list of physicians puppeteers are lawyers. This is a true story: when I was a pharmaceutical rep back in South Carolina, there was an attorney who was known to routinely sneak into the hospital and go from patient room to patient room handing out cards, telling the patient, "I sue doctors for a living." I am not saying that all lawyers are immoral, unscrupulous, unethical, and slimy. I know of at least two who do not fit any of those categories. If you give me a moment, I will try to remember their names. Sorry, their names escape me.

To legally protect himself, the average physician must practice defensive medicine. The only physicians out there not practicing defense medicine are those who have not been sued or have not been involved in a lawsuit. It is stupid to say "I am only going to do what I feel is right for my patient and ignore everything else that could possibly come back to bite me in the butt later legally."

While it is clear you can do the right thing and be sued anyway, it still follows that it is in our best interest to do as many right things as possible—even overkill—to protect ourselves legally. Doing more to protect yourself legally may not prevent the lawsuit, but it just may limit the amount of money you have to pay out in settlement or improve your chances of winning your case in court. Personally I have not yet been sued. However, most physicians will be sued at least once in their careers. So I am sure that my time is coming.

Let me tell you about a physician and patient encounter that will best illustrate the tough decisions a physician has to face regularly and the consequences of making a best educated guess that still has a bad outcome and ends up in litigation. A doctor was taking care of a gentleman over forty who had hypertension, an irregular heartbeat, and chronic renal failure. This was a man who rarely went to the doctor. He also had a propensity for not taking his medicine as prescribed. The doctor developed a relationship with the patient and saw him often to reinforce the reasons he had to take his medicines as prescribed; literally, it was a matter of life and death.

The doctor arranged for home healthcare to go out and actually put medicine in a pillbox for his patient. One day the patient went to see his doctor, a blood test was done, and one of the blood levels came back low. Since the blood thinning level was low, the right thing to do was increase the dose of his blood-thinning medicine. If it was that easy, our story would be over. The dilemma is this: was his therapeutic level low because he was taking too low a dose of medicine, or was his therapeutic level low because he was not taking his medication as prescribed?

With some patients, one has no real way of knowing. Even by asking we cannot be 100 percent sure we are getting accurate answers. More times than not, noncompliant patients say they are taking their medication. When you ask the color, the shape, or the dose of the medication they have a blank look on their faces. The patient I was telling you about *said* he was taking his medication.

If the patient's dose was not increased and the patient developed a clot that lead to a stroke, the doctor could potentially face a lawsuit since it could be argued that it was a sub-therapeutic dose of blood thinner that led to the formation of a clot in the heart that then caused the stroke.

If the doctor raised the dose of blood thinner and the patient had a brain bleed, the doctor could be sued because a lawyer would argue that the blood thinner dose should not have been increased, because the doctor knew his patient had a history of noncompliance and the doctor risked his patient having a brain hemorrhage by increasing the dose of blood thinner. Yet there is something else: this patient had other health issues. His hypertension, if not controlled, could lead to a massive brain hemorrhage.

The doctor believed what his patient told him and raised the dose of the blood thinner. A few weeks later, the patient suffered a massive cerebral hemorrhage and died. Why did this patient have a hemorrhage? Did the patient not take his blood pressure medication and so cause his brain hemorrhage? Did the doctor overshoot the blood-thinning level, which precipitated the bleed? Did the patient take his medicine incorrectly? The patient's wife sued the doctor for overshooting the blood-thinning level. This doctor had done everything he could for his patient but now faced a lawsuit. Doing all you can for a patient unfortunately doesn't matter anymore. It is all about the potential money. Unfortunately there are patients with the eager assistance of attorneys who see physicians as a lottery ticket.

This case did what most cases do; it settled out of court. The biggest problem the doctor had was limited documentation in the chart on why he did what he did. He explained all he did but couldn't back up all of his statements, because he did not having sufficient notes. No other doctors had seen this patient, and so there was no other support or corroboration to help defend his treatment.

Even though the doctor felt comfortable in defending his actions, he settled because he did not want to go through a drawn-out legal process and trial and face further potential personal exposure. After that experience the physician became overly cautious and made it a habit to order many supportive tests, over-document, and make many referrals to sub-specialists, even though he really didn't need them, doing all this in order to avoid future litigation.

Although sometimes it doesn't matter how careful one is, one can still be sued. Since hearing about this case, I also err on the side of caution and insist on backup. When someone wants to come talk to me about over-prescribing tests or excessive documentation—or excessive follow-up visits or excessive precautionary hospitalizations—I tell them to go jump in the lake. The risk of a potential lawsuit is just not worth it.

I am not saying that doctors do not make mistakes; we do. But no other industry is held to the same standard that we are held to. The fact is, when we err, someone may die. No amount of "I'm sorry" can soothe the tender soul of a family member who tragically loses a loved one because of a physician's error in judgment. Someone has to pay. That is what malpractice insurance is for. Money cannot bring a loved one back, but it does make going forward with life more bearable. Unfortunately some lawyers exploit vulnerable families by not just blurring but obliterating the line between a true malpractice case and a fishing expedition.

The goal of malpractice attorneys is not to take the case to court. It is to find as many potential mistakes as possible and force a settlement. The truth is I could virtually go through every medical chart in a physician's office or hospital and determine a different way that the patient could have been treated. That job is left for sellout medical expert physicians, experts who are paid to say whether their colleague potentially could have made a mistake, could have handled the situation another way, or might have taken another step in order to avoid a potential problem.

I actually did some chart review for malpractice plaintiffs' attorneys. I had to determine whether there was a case. I could have found something wrong with almost every single file I looked at. When push came to shove, I could have really come up with some creative reasons as to where a physician went wrong. I was actually quite good at it.

I stopped after three cases. I never testified in court and I made it clear to the plaintiff attorneys that I only reviewed charts. I would never sign an affidavit against another physician or testify against a physician. Why? "There, but for the grace of God, go I." After those three cases, I was uncomfortable even reviewing charts and I stopped.

It now seems that there are particular individuals who want to attack physicians on another legal front, criminalizing them for medical errors! Unbelievable! If society ever moves in that direction, look for a significant number of doctors to give up, myself included. I cannot imagine, after my best effort to care for a patient and making an unfortunate mistake, having to face criminal charges for the incident. I will not put my family in such jeopardy.

There used to be a time when pharmaceutical companies, insurance companies, hospitals, and even lawyers had some respect for physicians, but those days are now gone.

I never experienced Shangri-La as a physician, but I actually have heard that a physicians' Shangri-La once existed. It was a place where they were well respected by their community—by the insurance companies, hospitals, pharmaceutical companies—and wonder of wonders, where they were actually paid what the statements indicated. I guess you can't miss what you never had. It sure sounds like a nice place, though.

The ironic thing is that physicians have everything at their disposal to control almost every aspect of healthcare. We have a collective goal, which is patient care. We write all the orders that trigger almost two trillion dollars of annual healthcare expenditures. We have the personal financial resources.

There are approximately eight hundred thousand physicians in the United States.[11] Let us take 75 percent of that number, or 600,000 physicians. Multiply 600,000 by an average annual physician salary of $150,000 and you have a total of $90 billion a year in financial resources. If we contributed 1 percent of our income, or $1,500 annually, we would have $900 million a year to lobby our issues in Washington. Move over Big Insurance, Big Pharmaceuticals, and Big Bar Association; there would be a new sheriff in Washington. While I cannot speak for all my colleagues, I believe we can all find $125 a month, or the price of a daily cup of coffee at Starbucks, to take back healthcare. All we need is strong leadership.

Medicine has boomed in all areas in the last twenty years: areas such as medications, procedures, tests, medical equipment, techniques, and knowledge. As a physician you are inundated on a daily basis with volumes of paperwork and new drugs. Trying to stay on top of things that directly relate to our profession makes it very hard to be shrewd business people and sharp negotiators.

While we improved our knowledge so we could better serve our patients, every other player in the healthcare arena has sharpened their game. Hospitals, insurance companies, pharmaceutical companies, and lawyers—all via their lobbyists—have used the government to reconstruct the healthcare system without us.

Doctors on call overnight at a hospital are obligated to take care of uninsured patients. If a patient presents to the emergency room with chest pain that turns out to be a heart attack and winds up in the ICU for weeks, the physicians that take care of him do so for free. The doctor can bill the patients, but most of the time their fees are not collected. The patient of course also reserves the right to sue their doctors if they are unsatisfied with their treatment or outcome.

In this scenario, insurance companies are not on the hook and the hospital receives compensation for the state for care of the uninsured. The pharmaceutical companies get paid for the drugs used by this patient. The physician that saves the life gets nothing. On the other hand, in Atlanta a person named Brian Nichols is in jail preparing for trial charged with multiple murders. The bill for his defense, paid by tax payers, is almost $2 million; the case has not even gone to trial yet. Lawyers get paid, hospitals get paid, drug companies get paid, and everyone gets paid except physicians.

Well, McFly, sticking our heads in the sand will not work anymore. It never did. Physicians need to get in the game before we reach a point when we have no influence at all in the future of healthcare. A line in the sand has to be drawn, and McFly, *do not* back down this time!

# CHAPTER VI
# HOSPITALS
## Cost-Containment to the Death

What is the common link that binds most hospitals together? It is profitability, and the "cost-cutting" and "cost-containment" that ensures that profitability. Patients are pushed out of their beds way too soon, while senior hospital executives make millions of dollars in salary and bonuses.

There was a time when a hospitals' missions was primarily to take care of the sick, not be a profit mega center. Those hospitals never turned away the poor, didn't force patients out of a hospital bed, and didn't tell doctors who they could or could not admit. In the name of so-called cost-containment, it has become more of a profit issue and less of a concern for individuals in poverty. When choosing between a program that benefits the patient versus a program that improves the bottom line, the profitable program will always come first for hospitals.

Hospitals make money based on two principles: admissions and procedures. If you are an OB-GYN, hospital administrators encourage you to perform as many procedures or as many deliveries as possible in their hospital. If you are a surgeon, the hospital administration does its best to encourage you to perform as many surgical procedures in their hospitals as possible. If you are a family physician or internist, the hospital encourages you to admit as many patients as possible.

As a young physician just starting out, I was given an opportunity by a Tenet hospital in Atlanta to open an office in one of their professional buildings, across the street from the hospital. I was offered a two-year agreement to help me start my practice. I jumped at the opportunity because I knew that I wanted to be in private practice, and if someone else was willingly to pay the cost of getting me started, that would be great.

Tenet was not giving me this opportunity out of the kindness of its heart. It was counting on two things: first, I would admit my patients to its hospital, and second, I would refer my patients to sub-specialists who used its hospitals. Tenet didn't lose any money in this deal. In the end the investment it made in me paid off quite well.

I was a good corporate citizen for Tenet. When it wanted to expand into another county with its hospital system, I was invited to stand with the company down at the Georgia state capitol in support of the expansion. When town hall meetings were held in the county in question, the county in which I resided, I attended those meetings and spoke very favorably of the Tenet hospital system. I had admitting privileges at other hospitals in the Atlanta area, but essentially all my admissions went to Tenet hospitals.

When the executives of my hospital asked that I participate in an indigent-care project that would allow elderly people in assisted-living housing near the hospital access to primary care, I gladly chose to be a part of that project. I was a brand new primary-care physician. I had recently graduated from the Morehouse School of Medicine, Department of Family Practice. I relished the opportunity to take care of these patients. That was exactly what I trained to do at Morehouse. Initially I only saw about 10 percent of the patients in the program (90 percent of the patients were going to the hospital-employed primary-care physicians).

We were happy for every patient we saw in the program. We were very attentive to their needs; we returned their telephone calls and we got them in for appointments and did not cancel appointments. If they needed additional services, we referred them to other physicians within the Tenet network. If they needed to be admitted, we admitted them to Tenet.

Over time the percent of patients we treated in this program grew. We went from managing 10 percent to managing 90 percent of the community patients. This outreach program was working well. We were seeing individuals who had not been to the doctor in several months or even in several years. These were the individuals with multiple medical issues: diabetes, hypertension, high cholesterol, anemia, previous history of stroke, and previous history of heart attack. Each patient had an average of three to five serious chronic medical issues. The primary challenge for us as physicians was not determining the medication regimen these patients needed; it was finding the right medication regimen that the patient could afford. We used generic drugs when we could, and when we could not, we supplied patients with samples. We thought everything was going well.

Atlanta Medical Center, the Tenet hospital, in my eyes was an absolute hero. I thought the hospital recognized that there was a problem with access for indigent patients who lived in the surrounding community and it had created a program to meet the needs of that community.

As time went on, things began to change. There were meetings I was invited to attend with individuals in the hospital's administration regarding the cost of the program. It was implied that the direct cost of the transportation component of the program was an issue. I explained that it was a needed program and that much good was being done in the community. I also explained that while the direct transportation piece might be an issue, the hospital had to have been receiving a benefit from the multiple referrals we made within in the system to other specialists, the number of patients admitted, and all the patients that had procedures performed in the hospital.

Though my points were considered, unfortunately those indirect financial benefits to the hospital were not quantified on the balance sheet. What could clearly be seen were the thousands of dollars they were spending monthly on the transportation component of the program. The hospital eventually cut all funding for transportation. To the benefit of our patients, the physicians in my group banded together with other physicians in the hospital and we decided to pay the monthly cost of transportation for these patients.

I learned a lesson and grew up quickly when it came to hospitals and business. I learned that maximum profitability was job one. To validate this point, I found out later that one of the main reasons the program was created in the first place was to capture a particular revenue stream, termed "out layers," that the hospital previously was not taking advantage of. This was a program through which the hospital could get federal dollars by accessing indigent patients in the community.

The program was working. Patients who before did not have access to healthcare were being seen. The hospital was not losing money with the program, but it wasn't making a killing either. Atlanta Medical Center cut off the program. Never mind the patients who would have been left stranded by its decision. In the long run, the hospital got the best of all worlds. It no longer funded the program; the physicians were doing that and the hospital still reaped all the benefits. Physicians lost revenue by funding the transportation piece of the indigent care program to keep that program alive, while the hospital increased revenue by gaining referrals, admissions, and procedures. Physicians think patient care; hospitals think profitability.

Hospitals push physicians to admit as many patients as possible. We get a regular report from the hospital about our admission numbers. That report is as subtle as a pastor handing a church member a report of how much money they put in the offering plate. Hospitals also push doctors to discharge patients as quickly as possible. Why? To maximize revenue. Every doctor out there can probably tell you about their individual run-ins with hospitals and administration when it comes to patient care. One situation stands out in my mind—one that, I believe, pretty much sums up the agenda of hospitals.

A few years ago, I had a patient. We will call her Mrs. Wilson. I met Mrs. Wilson in the hospital as a primary-care consultant after she had just gone through major lower-back surgery. Mrs. Wilson worked for a company in its administrative department. She had Blue Cross and Blue Shield health insurance coverage. Mrs. Wilson had a problem with her lower back and underwent a procedure to help her relieve the pain.

Complications of that procedure left her with an abscess (pus) in the lumbar portion of her lower back. The hospital had no problem taking care of Mrs. Wilson. After all, she had insurance. She spent several days in the hospital and then went home. She came to my office for a routine follow-up and eventually I became her primary-care physician.

She did not do well after the procedure, and although she attempted to return to her job several times, she was unable to go back permanently. Letters were written by the surgeon who drained the abscess, as well as by me, to her employer, requesting that she be allowed to go on long-term disability. The request was denied, since it is customary for most insurance companies to deny the first application for disability. The insurance companies continued to ask the surgeon and myself for additional supporting paperwork and documentation, and they continued to ask the patient for more paperwork and documentation.

This dragged on for quite a while. The long and the short of it is that eventually Mrs. Wilson was released from her employment. Non-employment meant no healthcare coverage. The issue of getting compensation for long-term disability was far from being settled.

I continued to see Mrs. Wilson for primary-care issues and, considering the circumstances, depression soon was added to her list of chronic medical issues. Several months later Mrs. Wilson's blood pressure started becoming uncontrollable. She came to the office one day complaining of headache, dizziness, and shortness of breath. I checked her blood pressure, which was 210/120. She said she was taking her blood pressure medicines at home. Normal blood pressure is a reading less than 140/90.

Concerned about her symptoms and her high blood pressure, I quickly wrote admission orders and had one of my MAs (medical assistants) call the hospital to arrange a twenty-four-hour bed for my patient. While she called and I was writing my orders, I asked another MA to locate a wheelchair so that we could wheel Mrs. Wilson across the walkway and into the hospital's admissions office. In a short while, my MA came back and told me that the hospital was not going to allow me to admit her. Naturally I asked for the reason. The response was "she doesn't have any insurance."

I became very angry. I picked up the telephone and I called the hospital emergency room department myself and spoke to the charge nurse there. I told them about my patient. I told them about the fact that she was having concerning symptoms. I told them that the patient lived by herself and I was concerned about sending her home without first adequately controlling her blood pressure. The charge nurse said, "She does not have insurance and there are other hospitals that can take care of her." I was told I should put her in a taxi, and if I was very concerned, I should call an ambulance and have her taken to the county hospital. I had no privileges at that county hospital and she did not want to go to that hospital.

I decided to treat the high blood pressure as aggressively as possible in my office. After a couple of hours, Mrs. Wilson's blood pressure started going down and she felt a little better. I asked her if she felt well enough to drive home, she said yes. I gave her my cell number and said she could go home. I told her to check her blood pressure every few hours and call me with the results. I also told her to make sure her son or her neighbor stayed with her overnight, just in case. She called me a couple of times that evening, later that night, and the following morning. She did well, fortunately.

To be honest, I thought that if this approach did not go well, I would have opened myself to major liability. I could hear the plaintiff's attorney now: "Dr. Bennett, if you were so concerned about your patient's wellbeing, despite the fact that your patient did not want to go to the county hospital, you should have called an ambulance and send her there anyway." I did not send her to the county hospital, because I trusted my patient to follow my instructions. This was an instance of a physician doing what he thought was right, not what was legally most protective.

Getting back to the hospital's decision not to allow me to admit my patient because she did not have insurance: this was a hospital that in prior months, when she had insurance, had received her with open arms. Once her insurance benefits were gone, she was not their concern. Physicians think patient care; hospitals think profitability.

Large medical centers are not alone in looking at their bottom line. Some community hospitals are no better. After I completed step three of my medical board exams, I applied for and was granted a medical license from the state of Georgia. I was still a resident, but as a licensed physician, I could moonlight.

Boy, did I moonlight in residency! I was all over the place. I worked nights, weekends, in and out of town. I worked for hospitals, clinics, mental institutions. I did high school and college physicals. One could probably guess that I needed the money. I was married and now had two children; Danielle was six and Matthew was four.

I saw a lot of disgraceful things moonlighting. I worked at hospitals that struggled financially to keep their doors open, hospitals that hired nurses with suspended licenses because they could get them on the cheap, hospitals that lacked the needed equipment to treat critically ill patients but accepted these patients any way.

A fellow moonlighting resident told me about a case in a community hospital where we both worked. A woman who had only recently delivered a baby came into the hospital seizing. The patient was having convulsions and her airway had to be protected via intubation, or putting a tube down her throat to help her breathe. The initial attempts by the ER doctor to place the tube were not successful. Edema (swelling) occurred in the patient's throat, and it then became impossible to insert the tube. The patient now needed an emergency tracheotomy; in this procedure, the throat is cut and a tube is directly placed into the trachea. The ER did not have a suitable tracheotomy kit. No one had taken inventory that day. The patient died. She essentially choked to death. To save money this hospital had cut corners on equipment and staffing. That decision ended in tragedy.

I have personally experienced my own tragic outcomes in certain community hospitals that chose to cut corners. I am certainly not critical of all community hospitals. The majority of them do a good job. One probably receives more personal care if admitted to a small community hospital than compared to the mega chains. Unfortunately small community hospitals in underserved areas can be dangerous places, especially at night. These hospitals tend to be understaffed, have less qualified doctors, and more often than not are ill equipped. This should not come as a surprise. Underserved areas get the short end of the stick in all measurable areas of healthcare, so why should their hospitals be any different?

My tragic story begins about 3:00 a.m. one morning when I was paged to the ICU at a community hospital in the inner city. A nineteen-year-old college student with diabetes had been admitted to the hospital earlier with diabetic ketoacidosis, a serious condition referenced earlier that if not treated was fatal. She was about to crash. She was unconscious and her heart rhythm was irregular. A finger-stick blood sugar level reflected a blood sugar level above 800. (A normal level would be less than 126.) She was cold, clammy, and obviously about to go into cardiac arrest.

I quickly looked through her chart and saw that she was on the proper protocol for her condition. Why was she in trouble? I called a nurse in the ICU and instructed her to give the patient certain drugs to reverse her condition before she arrested. I also wanted to prepare for intubation. The nurse could not administer the medication, because her license was suspended and only her supervisor could administer the medications. Her supervisor was on the floor and was called. One has to ask the question, why was the nurse with the suspended license in the ICU while the nurse supervisor was on the floor, and not the other way around?

Finally the supervisor made it to the ICU and administered the drugs. The young lady went into cardiac arrest anyway. We tried to resuscitate her but were unsuccessful. Her underlying condition had overwhelmed her. This was a young lady who, hours earlier, was alert and talking. She was now dead. What happened?

I went back into her room and saw a piece of the puzzle. Her IV bag of insulin was on the floor, not hung on the post as it should have been. Somehow it had been knocked down and no one noticed. The other piece of the puzzle was in the chart and medical record. The correct orders were written, but the nurse did not follow the established protocol as written. In essence the patient received no treatment for her critical condition. The nurse said she was busy doing something else. I was furious. I confronted her. She walked away to the other side of the ICU. Hospitals: cost-containment to the death.

# CHAPTER VII
# PHARMACEUTICAL AND HEALTH INSURANCE COMPANIES
## WWE Tag Team Wrestling at Its Best

For years drug and health insurance company stocks have been some of the most highly recommended investments on Wall Street. Their profitability has been nothing short of incredible. Their senior executives have received tens of millions of dollars in bonuses. All this while there are millions of Americans without healthcare insurance and without the means to purchase needed medications.

Even though most major drug breakthroughs occur in the United States, pharmaceutical companies charge more for drugs here in America than in other countries. Why do they do this? The simple answer is, because they can. There are government drug-pricing regulations in other countries and little price regulation in the U.S. There is also a "virtual drug price" game played by the pharmaceutical industry on both the American public and doctors. What is the name of this virtual-pricing game? How is it played? It's called the co-pay game.

The average patient believes the price of a drug is the co-pay they pay at the pharmacy. Doctors also fall for this trap. Pharmaceutical reps try to play this game with me all the time. They say, "Dr. Bennett, this drug is tier two on most insurance and will only cost your patients twenty dollars." Sounds good.

What the average patient does not know, and what the reps neglect to tell doctors, is that the total cost of the drug may be as high as $250 per month. Many reps don't tell physicians the true retail cost of the drugs they sell, because they don't know the cost themselves. Their instructions are to market their drug based on co-pay, not the drug's true cost. The patient pays the twenty-dollar co-pay and their health insurance company picks up the rest. That really means that the *patient* picks up the rest by paying higher insurance premiums.

There is no deal here. There is no free lunch, just (in my attempt to be less contentious) "creative marketing" by the pharmaceutical companies who pass the cost through the health insurance industry to the general public. It's like WWE tag team wrestling. The pharmaceutical and insurance companies are beating the crap out of the public in the ring, while their lobbyist, the paid-off referee, distracts the public's manager, the U.S. government.

The second "con" (now I *am* being confrontational) that drug companies have used over the years for the outrageous cost of drugs has been that they have "reinvested millions of dollars into research and development"—a plausible rationalization. While drug companies *do* reinvest sufficient dollars into research and development, doing so is obviously self-serving, since development of newer drugs means more opportunity for more profit. A drug company that doesn't reinvest in research and development is a dead drug company, since in a few years their front-line products hit the generic market. Let the U.S.

auto industry try to tell the public that U.S.-made cars cost more because the industry has to put significant dollars back into research and development. The U.S. public has a counter to that argument; it's called Toyota.

I know a lot about the pharmaceutical industry since I once was a rep in the industry. *I* used to tell doctors about co-pays and the millions of dollars spent on research and development. It was a fantastic job. I was twenty-two years old. I was well paid. I had a company car. I had full benefits. I attended meetings in different cities. I stayed at nice hotels. I was living the good life.

At annual sales meetings, or whenever a new drug came to market, we were pumped up with the value our products had for society. I have been sarcastic about the pharmaceutical industry, but to be honest, some of the drugs that come to market *are* breakthroughs and are very important. One of the drugs I sold was Vasotec, a blood pressure medicine. Vasotec proved not only to be effective in lowering blood pressure but also had positive effects on patients with congestive heart failure or a history of heart attacks. It also helped to preserve the kidney function of diabetics.

Vasotec cost about thirty dollars per month then. A drug of that significance today costs about four times that. Why? Does the average new car cost four times what it did twenty years ago? Has the price of a loaf of bread or a gallon of milk quadrupled in the last twenty years? So why have drug prices quadrupled? Simply because "the market" allows it. Our third-party payer system allows the pharmaceutical industry to charge whatever it wants; our health insurance company pays it and then raises our premiums to cover the cost. Our employers decrease the percentage they cover on our health insurance, and we end up paying more for healthcare. And you thought that all that drug cost you was a twenty-dollar co-pay. Think again.

One of the most outrageous examples of ridiculous drug-price gouging is drugs used to prevent osteoporosis in women. Osteoporosis is a disease that causes bones to become brittle and subject to fracture. This condition occurs mostly in postmenopausal women. With the limited benefits of calcium and vitamin D therapy, and the cancer concerns regarding the use of estrogen in women to treat this disease, a newer class of drugs, called the anti-resorptive bisphosphonates, has been quite effective in the treatment and preventing osteoporosis.

In this class there is a once-a-day drug named Actonel. I called a few local pharmacies and found out the cost of Actonel is about $105 per month for a thirty-day supply, or $3.50 per pill. Boniva is a pill in the same class that is taken once a month. Does Boniva cost $3.50 per pill? Boniva costs about $105 per pill. The pharmaceutical company would say that the convenience of once-a-month dosing of Boniva when compared to once-a-day dosing of Actonel makes it cost-effective. Baloney. They are just trying to maximize profits at an accelerated rate. Roche is selling the heck out of Boniva. Big-time marketing on TV for Boniva has led to big-time sales of over $400 million in 2006.[12] Do the math. A one-year supply of Actonel, 365 pills, costs $1,260. A one-year supply of Boniva, 12 pills, costs $1,260, yet we will pay it. Why not? The co-pay is only twenty dollars. Amazing.

I am not a socialist. I consider myself as much of a capitalist as the next guy. I believe pharmaceutical companies should try to make all the profit they can, but the bulk of those profits should not be made on the backs of Americans. Get your money from other countries that have a limited drug industry or none at all—countries that invest no money in pharmaceutical research and development. Make foreign countries pay more for their drugs. Don't gouge them; just charge them more. Give Americans a break, please!

Pharmaceutical industry profitability is an area where physicians can take an active role in policing costs. We do not have to prescribe the high-priced drugs that we see advertised on television for routine medical problems when instead we can prescribe several generics that are safe and effective. If we as physicians stuck to our guns and, in an effort to force down the prices of trade-name drugs, prescribed the generic equivalents, we would be successful. Not one pill is prescribed if we do not write for it. That is powerful.

Still, I've got to hand it to the pharmaceutical industry. Marketing, marketing, marketing! Marketing to physicians in the office, marketing to physicians in medical magazines, marketing directly to the consumer on television or radio.

Heart disease and stroke are two of the leading causes of death in America.[13] Risk factors for these diseases include hypertension, diabetes, and hypercholesterolemia. There are generic drugs on the market to treat these diseases at one-third the cost of trade-name drugs. We need to prescribe more of these drugs and less of the trade-name drugs whenever applicable.

We now obviously prescribe a mother load of trade medicines, which is why the pharmaceutical industry is so outrageously profitable. Unfortunately many of us do so because it is a convenient, quick thing to do. We see a patient with hypertension, we run to the drug cabinet, pull out a week's or a month's worth of samples, tell the patient to try it, and if there are no side effects and their blood pressure comes under control, we write a prescription on their next visit and we move on.

More times than not, a generic drug would have had the same benefit, and at a much lower cost.

Again, give the pharmaceutical industry credit, they have an amazingly strong lobbying organization. They stand to make a killing with the implementation of Medicare part D. Medicare part D is the prescription-drug plan for seniors that has the government picking up the cost of medications. In the past Medicare benefits included only office visits and hospitalization, not medication.

Personally I believe Medicare part D is revolutionary. In the past I have seen seniors who had to choose between buying food or purchasing their medication. Some seniors would try to take daily medications every other day in an effort to save money. Mind you, I am in favor of a senior prescription drug plan. I simply could not believe Congress passed this bill, knowing that the cost of the program, over a ten-year period, would be more than $500 billion, *and they did not demand price regulation.*

Suppose a company named Coffee Depot sold one million pounds of coffee beans per year to several customers. One new customer comes along who wants to buy one million pounds of coffee beans from Coffee Depot annually, virtually doubling Coffee Depot's revenue overnight. Coffee Depot then tells this new customer that they will sell the new customer the coffee beans, but the customer must pay the same rate, and in some cases a higher rate, as smallest customer pays.

If you were the new customer, wouldn't you want discount pricing? The smart business decision would be to insist upon discount pricing. So why did the government agree to forgo discount pricing from drug companies when it came to Medicare part D? That move is especially strange since the government already engaged in discount pricing for drugs they get through the Veterans Administration.

Getting a bill of this financial magnitude passed without discount pricing reflects in bright light the power of the pharmaceutical lobby groups. In fact, several Medicare executives, as well as powerful congressional representatives, whom you would think would be trying to make the best deal possible for the American taxpayer, actively worked to push through the bill. Within months, for some within weeks after the passage of the bill, these Medicare executives and a congressman left their former posts for extremely lucrative job opportunities within the pharmaceutical industry.

How blatant can you be? People should be looking at jail time for this sham. Physicians will be prescribing a lot more trade-named drugs and the government will pay for them and further increase the profitability of the drug companies, with no regulation or cost-containment by Congress. Let me give you a stock tip: buy all the pharmaceutical stock you can.

If drug companies cannot make enough money from known major-disease processes, they'll just market rare-disease processes in order to make major dollars. Restless leg syndrome and dry eye disease are rare, but today we see commercial after commercial during the evening news about these conditions. As a primary-care physician, I can count but a hand full of people I have treated in the last ten years with a true diagnosis of restless leg syndrome or dry eye disease. If you believe the ads, you'd assume these were diseases I see every day.

The king of "hype-disease" marketing, though, is the marketing for sexual impotence. Sildenafil was a drug developed for pulmonary arterial hypertension, but the drug had a worrisome side effect; it prolonged erections. That side effect became a fix for sexual impotence *and* a multi-billion dollar product. Sildenafil became Viagra, the blue pill. Now you know the rest of the story. I wouldn't be surprised if the number of prescriptions written in this country for the three male enhancement products is ten times that of the true number of men with sexual impotence. Men who do not need a pill for erectile dysfunction get these pills prescribed routinely. Ah, the beauty of hype marketing!

Drug-company lobby groups have also done an excellent job in preventing Americans from getting drugs from Canada or other countries that have a strong track record for exporting drugs. The government will say getting drugs from overseas is a safety issue. I tell you it's a U.S. pharmaceutical price-protection issue. More people die each year in this country from eating imported fruit than die from imported drugs from reputable countries.[14] I don't see anyone running out to ban imported strawberries. If you want to curb the cost of prescription medicine in this country, the government should allow free trade of prescription pharmaceuticals with proper controls for safety.

The pharmaceutical industry still has us over the barrel; there are several areas of medicine without generic substitutes, and as consumers, we will continue to pay excessively for those medications. Several of them could save your life, but only if you can afford them. If you can't, you die.

By the way, drug companies will say they have special programs for the uninsured or those that do not have medications. You simply go to your doctor, have the necessary forms filled out, and get the medication. Sounds good on the surface, doesn't it? To prescribe a medication for a patient, I simply have to write a prescription. The patient then picks up their medication at the pharmacy. That is it.

For a patient to participate in the free-drug programs offered by most pharmaceutical companies, at least one form has to be completed, partly by the patient and partly by the physician. Some forms want you to send in a prescription; some don't. Some will send you a one-month supply, and then you have to renew the form every month. Some drug manufacturers want the medication delivered to the doctor's office, and others will send it directly to the patient. Get the picture? A physician *can* get medication from a pharmaceutical company for needy patients, but the process is usually tedious, complicated, and needs constant renewals.

I am not impressed with the efforts of the pharmaceutical industry regarding its effort to provide medication for those who cannot afford it. To impress me they need to simplify the process of getting the medication to the indigent, *reduce* the price of medications to Americans, and *increase* overseas pricing to make up the gap in lost revenues.

Health insurance companies do not get a free pass either. They have a great three-prong marketing plan: (1) insure only healthy people; (2) if you have a controllable chronic disease, insure you, but have you pay through the nose for premiums; (3) really sick people get no insurance at all. What is that plan worth? It is worth tens of billions for insurance reserve deposits, while 18,000 people die each year because they were uninsured. What a business model!

Even though I said before that I am a capitalist, I also believe players in the healthcare industry should not be allowed to make billions of dollars by deciding who will live and who will die. That is exactly what health insurance companies are deciding. Who will live? The people they choose to insure. Who will die? The people they leave out in the cold. Let me make it crystal clear. As a physician, if faced with two people bleeding to death, neither ethically nor morally would I only stop the bleeding for the person who would pay my bill. How could I do that? How could I let the other person just die?

Yet, day in and day out, health insurance companies deny people with preexisting health conditions coverage. These are people with cancer, heart disease, and stroke, any of which could be death sentences if not properly treated. Yet insurance is denied. Worse than that, people who have been paying premiums for years and develop cancer, heart disease, or stroke find their insurance companies doing all they can to deny claims. People have fought their insurance companies up to the day they die for coverage of certain treatment options. The system is broken. We must fix it.

In closing this chapter, let me say this: as Americans we cannot have it both ways. We cannot wail against the profitability of pharmaceutical and health insurance companies, then dump the stocks of companies in these industries should they lower prices or premiums and their stock value goes down. We can't complain about the decreased worth of our stock portfolios if there is more price regulation. We are going to need to make a choice. As with everything else in life, there is no free lunch.

# CHAPTER VIII
# MEDICAL EDUCATION Part 1
## America Will Need a Lot More Doctors

A little-known fact to the American public is that the United States is expected to have a physician shortage of somewhere between 100,000 and 200,000 by the year 2020.[15] After more than a decade of denying that there would be any shortage of physicians in the future, the American Medical Association called for a 15 percent increase in the number of medical student graduates by the year 2015; a number that has recently been increased to 30 percent. Even under ideal circumstances, if that request was implemented by all U.S. medical schools, there would still not be enough new physicians trained to meet the projected need.

The medical school side of the equation is only one side of future medical education concerns; every medical student has to get additional medical residency training after graduation to become eligible for licensure to practice medicine in the United States. Currently there are approximately one hundred thousand residency positions in the United States. The cost of training one medical resident is approximately $100,000 per year.[16] The total annual cost for medical resident education then would be approximately $10 billion. The funding for medical residency training primarily comes from Medicare. Funding also comes from the Veterans Administration (VA).

There was a cap placed in the mid-'90s on increasing the number of residency positions because of the projected "surplus" of physicians. The cap would of course have to be adjusted upward to meet the demand for more residency training positions in the next fifteen years. But once again, increasing the number of residents places further burdens on the budget of Medicare and the Veterans Administration system. If medical schools doubled their number of graduates, another $10 billion per year would be needed for medical residency training. Considering the current funding struggles of Medicare and the VA, where is the money going to come from?

One may ask how we got ourselves in this position to begin with. We can start is in the mid-'90s when the American Medical Association accepted a prediction that there would be a future surplus of physicians by 2000.[17] In fact, the opposite has occurred. The number of first-year MDs enrolled per one hundred thousand of population has declined since the 1980s.[18] In the 1980s the U.S., for all intents and purposes, stopped opening new medical schools. Now, as the U.S. population increases, baby boomers are reaching senior-citizen status, demanding more medical resources; senior physicians are retiring; and new physicians want to work fewer hours.[19] So that prediction of a surplus of physicians was woefully "inaccurate," to say the least. All discussions and proposals on the table surrounding the pending physician demand have to be entertained.

Approximately 25 percent of the physicians practicing in the United States are international medical graduates or foreign medical graduates.[20] These are medical students or doctors who trained abroad, then applied to U.S. residency programs. Once their programs were completed, they became physicians licensed to practice United States. Most studies show that international medical graduates are more likely to practice in underserved areas such as inner cities and rural counties than their American counterparts are.

When looking at primary-care specialties, recent data also indicates that almost 50 percent of the IMG (international medical graduates) chose careers in primary care compared to approximately 30 percent of U.S. medical school graduates. International medical graduates face serious obstacles and the perception of inferior training (and therefore competency) by hospitals, residency directors, and patients. International medical students or physicians with heavy accents have added difficulty being accepted by patients and the general medical community. The bottom line, though, is we need them. Currently U.S. medical schools produce more than six thousand too few doctors for available residency positions. International medical doctors fill approximately 25 percent, or 6,000 slots, of the available residency positions each year.[21]

The greatest obstacle international medical graduates face is not having adequate U.S. clinical experience. Most have finished medical school and residency in a foreign country and have no real U.S. clinical experience in the outpatient or inpatient setting. Lack of U.S. clinical experience means lack of familiarity with equipment used in hospitals, U.S. patient culture, administrative paperwork, and the standard protocols that are followed by U.S. medical school graduates.

Because of a perception of "patient safety," international medical doctors have a difficult time finding private physicians or hospitals that would be willing to allow them access to patients, which would enable the foreign medical graduate to gain the clinical experience necessary prior to applying to U.S. residency programs. As with U.S.

students, an attending or teaching physician must supervise and teach international medical students during a clinical rotation or clerkship. But unfortunately, as stated earlier, there are not enough attending physicians or hospitals willing to give the foreign-trained student doctor a chance to learn in a real clinical setting.

There is a perception of harm to the public when referring to foreign-trained medical doctors, even though many of those doctors have successfully passed the same medical board exams as their U.S. counterparts. Many of these foreign-trained doctors also practiced for years in their country of origin prior to coming to the United States, giving them more real-world experience than new U.S. doctors just out of medical school. Yet as a group they are essentially considered "less than" in U.S. medical circles. If one speaks to some of the foreign-trained doctors who have been successful, they will tell you how much harder they felt they had to work to gain the respect of their U.S. peers.

The story is no different from the perception of blacks being intellectually inferior to whites. To get past the negative perceptions, blacks of previous generations had to work harder to prove their worth. There are some that will argue that is still the case. This is the current plight of a foreign-trained doctor who wants to practice in America. To make public perception worse, it seems media has no reservations about sensationalizing a negative story that involves foreign-trained doctors. I have been in medicine as a student, resident, or practicing physician for sixteen years now. I cannot recall one news story in that time that focused on the value foreign-trained doctors have in this country. I guess that would not sell newspapers.

Foreign-born and -trained medical graduates are not the only individuals who attempt to come into the U.S. healthcare profession. There are

Americans who were not successful in getting into U.S. medical schools and go abroad for their medical education and wish to come back to the U.S. for residency.

Thousands of foreign-trained Americans gain acceptance to U.S. residency programs each year.[22] Offshore-trained Americans encounter the same problems as foreign individuals who attempt to come into the country to get into residency; they lack U.S. clinical training experience. They too have difficultly getting into hospitals to gain critical experience, without which they will not be viable candidates for residency.

A reasonable concern of hospitals is the standard of medical training the student received from his or her foreign medical program. There are approximately 1,900 medical schools in 172 countries around the world.[23] Standards differ in each country. One can easily see why residency directors are very skeptical and make every effort to avoid accepting international medical graduates into their programs if they are able to fill their positions with U.S. medical graduates.

However, as previously stated, there are not enough U.S. medical students going into primary-care specialties, thus making it imperative that international medical graduates fill the void. When the rubber meets the road and the predicted physician shortage becomes reality, especially in primary care, decisions in medical education we make today, which are exclusive instead of inclusive of foreign-trained doctors, will hurt all Americans dearly.

Over the past twenty years, a significant number of the U.S.-based medical school programs on Caribbean islands have come into being. To date almost every country in the Caribbean has a chartered U.S.-based medical school program. Most of the students that attend these programs are American citizens, permanent residents, or Canadian citizens who wish to practice medicine in the United States. They go abroad for two years to do their basic science or foundational years. Upon successful completion of their basic training, the majority choose to come back to the U.S. to complete their last two clinical years at U.S. hospitals.

The biggest problem with the majority of these schools is a lack of appropriate standards, appropriate clinical training after completion of basic science years, appropriately credentialed professors, and appropriate administrative leadership. Many of these schools are actually profit mills, but because the demand is so great, more and more Americans and Canadians find themselves flocking to these schools in order to become physicians. The biggest area of struggle for these students is once again the clinical phase of their education.

Many states have strict guidelines, mandating that clinical years be completed in teaching hospitals or hospitals that have U.S. medical students or residents training in them, but hospitals that meet that criteria are few and far between. There is a requirement by some residency programs and states that student rotations be verified by someone either in the medical educational or medical staff department of the hospital where the rotation took place. That type of verification has also proved very difficult to get for internationally trained students.

Many unscrupulous Caribbean programs merely attach their students to physicians and essentially try to sneak the students into the hospitals without going through proper channels. This type of procedure creates a liability situation for the hospital because the student circumvents the hospital's credentialing process for all medical personnel who use the hospital for training. This credentialing is not only for student doctors but also for nurses, medical assistants, and others involved in patient care.

During the credentialing orientation, issues such as JAHCO requirements, HIPPA compliance, accidental needle sticks, and hospital codes are discussed; badges are issued. The orientation is clearly important, but many doctors who take students circumvent the system and take the student into the hospital without the knowledge of the administration.

Most would agree there has to be a significant overhaul of the current Caribbean medical school system. At the same time, U.S. hospitals need to find a way to accommodate properly trained international students. If they did, students would not have to use a back-door approach to gaining critical clinical hospital experience. Being understaffed is a chief complaint of hospitals. These students can provide these institutions with the additional hands necessary to meet patient needs. All that is required is for hospital administrators and medical educators to make the effort to think outside the box and make the student a resource and not a liability.

All the major American medical school administrations or associations, such as the American Medical Association (AMA), the American Association of Medical Colleges, and the Liaison Committee on Medical Education (LCME), have to make a decision on how to deal appropriately with internationally trained students regardless of their native country. Shutting these students out of hospital training is not a reasonable option, considering we are going to need a significant number of doctors sooner rather than later. That is simply an undeniable fact. We will principally need more doctors in primary-care specialties; this is again an undeniable fact. We need to use all the resources at our disposal to increase the number of physicians in the United States without permitting a decrease in the quality of patient care.

As I stated earlier, the fact that the AMA has a plan to increase the total number of medical student enrollments by 30 percent is admirable, but there are issues with that plan. The first and primary issue is where the money will come from to fund this increase. It costs approximately $100,000 a year to train one medical student. If the current U.S. medical schools were able to increase enrollment by five thousand, it would be an added burden of approximately $500 million dollars per year for training, and that is just for five thousand additional students in year one. By year four there would be 20,000 additional students in training, now costing $2 billion annually. Remember, the shortage is expected to be between 100,000 and 200,000 physicians. The proposed plan would graduate only an additional five thousand physicians per year. The numbers do not match up, and even if they did, the cost would be staggering.

What about building more medical schools in the U.S. to limit the need for internationally trained doctors? In other words, grow our own. Sounds good, but that plan would also be cost-prohibitive. There are currently 126 medical schools in the U.S.[24] The demand for the future would literally require opening another 120 schools. The cost of building one medical school can be as high as $450 million, which makes building a significant number of new schools to meet the need unrealistic and impractical.

At the turn of the century in the 1900s, there were more than a thousand U.S. medical schools with various standards: two- to four-year enrollment and very little post-medical-school training. Steps had to be taken to stabilize medical education. Eventually medical school programs were standardized to a four-year curriculum and stringent regulations. Today the number of accredited U.S. medical schools stands at 126. Now, in the first decade of the twenty-first century, we have to rethink U.S. medical education. We have to expand our current medical training facilities as much as we can afford to. We have to improve the opportunity for foreign-trained doctors to gain U.S. clinical experience without compromising patient care. We have to start thinking outside the box.

Let's explore another option, provider extenders known as nurse practitioners and physician assistants. Provider extenders receive medical training but not to the extent of an MD. The average MD receives an average of eight years of formal medical educational training, while an extender receives two to four years.[25] Most extenders work under the license of a physician and many cannot prescribe certain classes of drugs. I believe extenders will play a vital role in the future of medicine, especially in the field of primary care, but a medical doctor and a provider extender are not professional equals. We will need to solve our pending healthcare provider shortage primarily with physicians. I will further review the value of physician assistants and nurse practicitioners in the next chapter.

# CHAPTER IX
# MEDICAL EDUCATION Part 2
## Time to Think Outside the Box

What about non-accredited privately owned and operated medical schools? Schools that would not be regulated by U.S. accreditation bodies. Let's not ask the government to fund new schools; instead let's give private industry the opportunity to solve this shortage dilemma. Currently private investment groups own all the schools in the Caribbean. One only has to look across the board at every other professional discipline. There are private law schools, private universities, and private business schools, so why not private medical schools? Forget it.

It is illegal for any private entity to open or operate a medical school in the United States or in any United States territory. This policy was instituted to "protect the public" against dirty, filthy capitalists infiltrating the healthcare educational system. I can hear the argument now. "We can't have private investment training our doctors or we will merely revert to the problems medial education had in the early nineteenth century: too many profit-motivated medical schools without standards and regulations." Sounds like a reasonable position for our government to take, doesn't it? Let us take a closer look.

Private industry owns hospitals that manipulate patient care to maximize profit, and that's legal. Private industry owns health insurance companies that dictate treatment options to physicians to reduce costs and maximize profit, and that is legal. Private industry owns pharmacies that fill prescriptions and are profit-driven. Some pharmacies have their own medical clinics; you can see their provider, get a prescription, and get the prescription fill at in one place. Talk about vertical integration. How is there not a conflict of interest here? Nevertheless, this is legal.

However, let someone who wants to improve U.S. medical education open a medical school in Atlanta, Georgia, using the exact same curriculum and professors as U.S. medical schools, and they go to jail.

U.S. law does not allow a student to sit in a classroom in America for instruction for their first two years of book-based basic sciences via a private entity. It is, however, acceptable for that same student who completed their basic science years in another country via private enterprise to complete their two clinical years in the U.S. The clinical years are the years when there is patient contact. A student cannot study and read their medial books in a classroom here, but they can have patient contact once they have read their medical books and passed their classed abroad. What sense does that make? One would think it should be the other way around—that you could do your academic years in America and initial patient contact and clinical years would need to be abroad to "protect" U.S. patients—yet that is not the system. Let's explore "protecting the public" from foreign trained medical students. Foreign trained students, just like their U.S. counterparts participate in hands-on, patient contact, clinical rotations in hospitals today. To my knowledge their has been no greater incidence of inappropriate contact or conduct by these students compared to their U.S. peers.

Medical education academia and authorities must revisit these areas. It would be clearly easier now, given the technology advancements in communication and access, compared to the 1900s, to monitor private medical education. Having the programs here offers better and easier control and monitoring of standards of the curriculum, professors, and infrastructure of the basic sciences—control and monitoring that does not currently take place in foreign programs. Allowing private investors to initiate basic science programs in the United States would:

1. Improve the quality of students who attend these programs, since qualified students who do not get into medical school because of numbers would prefer completing their medical education in the U.S. and not overseas.

2. Improve the quality of the professors who teach these basic science courses.

3. Allow monitoring by state regulatory officials who can readily visit these institutions and ensure the following of guidelines.

4. Increase the number of doctors in states that have shortages by mandating that a student who attends a private U.S. medical school only be licensed in the state where they completed their education.

Many will tell you that only qualified students get into medical school and the students denied admission are academically inferior. That is not true. The standards for medical school admission are more of a supply-versus-demand issue. There are a lot of qualified applicants and very few slots. Add in nepotism, the "good old boy" network, and affirmative action, and the number of available slots diminishes further. More students would be accepted if more openings existed. The fact that the American Medical Association has asked medical schools to increase first-year enrollment by 30 percent is significant since it obviously shows that at least another 30 percent of medical school applicants would be admitted today if those spaces were available.

The opening of private medical schools should be a right of a state, since it is the state that suffers from the scarcity of physicians in rural, intercity, and other underserved areas. Encouraging private enterprise via economic incentives to start basic science programs in underserved states would ensure more doctors for that state, assuming the state granted a medical license that did not have reciprocity or transferability to other states.

Privately funded U.S. medial schools would have other advantages. To train one medical student is very expensive[26] and requires significant federal and state funding. There would be no burden on the U.S. taxpayer to pay for a private program.

Students in offshore programs receive privately funded financial aid to pay for their medical education; therefore, no tax dollars are spent for their education. When considering the AMA's plan to increase the number of U.S. medical graduates by 30 percent, this private medical education program allows us to increase the number of graduates by another 30 percent, giving us a better chance of stemming off the impending shortage of physicians. As illustrated before, it will be very expensive to try to increase the number of medical school enrollees or build enough new medical schools to meet the demand. A private medical school initiative offers an alternative.

If a privately funded medical program was created, the order of events would be as follows: a potential medical student first applies to a U.S.-accredited medical school program. If they are unsuccessful, going offshore or overseas to a non-accredited program would not be the only option. They could attend a non-accredited program in the United States. Currently foreign medical graduates from non-accredited schools are eligible for licensure in most states. Graduates of private medical schools would only be eligible to practice medicine in the state where they completed their medical education. Law has a similar program. There are non-accredited private law schools whose graduates are only eligible to practice in the state where they completed the program.[27] There should be a similar program for medical education.

If this private state medical school program was sanctioned, hospitals in the states would be more willing to accept students for clinical training because they would be assisting in the training of doctors that had a higher likelihood of joining their medical staff after training. Everyone wins in this scenario. Countries that badly need to keep their physicians would have less depletion of their doctors because fewer foreign medical graduates would be necessary. The majority of the unscrupulous Caribbean medical school programs would all dry up, as qualified students would seek their medical education from a U.S. state-sponsored medical school, or one of the remaining educationally sound Caribbean medical schools.

Keep in mind that not having a large pool of qualified applicants for medical school is not the issue. The issue is not having enough slots for those qualified applicants. Going to private medical school programs will give qualified American students a chance to realize their dreams of becoming physicians without having to go abroad. There is virtually no downside to this plan.

Unless there is an organized, focused plan to deal with the predicted physician shortage, one can predict that in fifteen years foreign physician recruitment will take the same route as foreign nurse recruitment. There will be an expedited visa process. There will be large broker firms going into several countries to recruit MDs and fast-track them into the U.S. system. The U.S. has already successfully clear-cut a significant number of nurses from developing and underserved countries. Fifteen years from now, we will be doing the same thing to supply the U.S. with doctors from other countries. We do not need to do that. There are steps we can take proactively, today, to prevent disaster.

I can say very confidently that a primary concern of all state medical boards in the United States is to ensure the quality of physicians before they are given the privilege to practice. The charge of state medical boards is to protect the public. With that in mind, the current system is set up such that all international medical students or graduates who wish to practice medicine in the United States have to go through a uniform credentialing process, which requires verification of critical medical educational documents, completion of U.S. licensure examinations, and completion of a residency in a particular area or specialty of interest.

It does not matter what country one is from or how many years one had spent in private practice. Every foreign-trained physician who wants to practice medicine in the U.S. must go through the same process, and that means repeating some or all of a medical residency. If we do not find reasonable ways to address the impending shortage of physicians, one wonders whether fifteen years down the road the quality and the standards for practicing medicine in the U.S. as a foreign-trained medical doctor will dramatically change in order to meet public demand. Will we have reached the point when it is no longer necessary for a foreign-trained physician to complete a three-year residency program before they can practice medicine in the U.S.?

We discussed earlier that the American Association of Medical Colleges plans to increase U.S. medical school enrollment by 30 percent, which will not make much of a dent in physician need. We also discussed that building enough new medical schools (we need at least another hundred) to meet the demand for physicians is extremely cost-prohibitive at a price tag of as much as $450 million per school. An increase in medical schools will require an increase in faculty. There are already concerns that just increasing medical school enrollment by 15 percent in the current medical school structure is creating a burden on basic science and clinical staff. Adding 100,000 medical students in the next fifteen years would create a scenario in which it would be difficult to maintain suitable teaching faculty. This is because U.S. medical schools have large numbers of faculty and staff in each department and require faculty to teach, do research and to publish. Non-accredited programs have fewer faculty per department and faculty's only obligation is to teach.

It has taken approximately eighty years to create the current medical school structure in the United States. As slowly as the medical community and the powers that control it move toward making any change, I really do not expect any dramatic or outside-the-box comprehensive solutions to the pending physician shortage from academia. As physicians we are routinely slow and methodical when making decisions. The answers to the shortage will be driven by an economic solution made by the corporate power brokers in business, and not by the academic power brokers in medicine.

We were forced into the health management organization (HMO) system by the economics of medicine. Gone are the days when a physician would see a patient, charge what they wanted, and receive payment. Gone also are the days when a physician could prescribe whatever drug they thought necessary without the involvement of an insurance company. Gone are the days when a physician could admit a patient to a hospital without first getting prior authorization from the insurance industry. There was a time when a patient could be admitted to the hospital a few days for tiredness.

While as a physician I can clearly state that I do not like the controls placed on me by the insurance industry regarding seeing patients, prescribing drugs, or admitting patients for hospitalization, it is hard to argue against the data. Corporate control of healthcare has slowed the annual percent increase in medical cost in the U.S. In a similar manner in which aggressive steps were taken to control health costs, we must take similar aggressive measures to stem the pending physician shortage in this country.

Other considerations that are put on the table regarding increasing the total number of providers are dramatically increasing the number of nurse practitioners or physician assistants and also expanding the prescription privileges of these individuals. While I believe that physician assistants (PAs) and nurse practitioners will play a vital role in expanding the number of providers in the area of primary care in the future, I cannot agree with limitless expansion of their scope of practice or their prescribing privileges. There is a reason it takes a minimum of seven years to become a board-eligible or a board-certified physician. It takes four years of medical school and then three to five years of residency to reach that plateau.

A new physician, who completed residency and has only a couple of years of experience, will tell you that private practice is quite a challenge, especially when it comes to making decisions on patient care without the safety net of an attending physician. Remember, these new doctors were once college students with 3.5+ GPAs before going to medical school and completing residency. These are individuals who endured the rigors of the MCAT, then the U.S. Medical Licensure Examination, (Step 1, then Step 2, then Step 3), and specialty board examinations. Even with all that education and training, they still sometimes question their capabilities when on their own.

There is no way the level of education, preparedness, or experience of a PA or nurse practitioner, who has gone through two to four years of total education, can be compared to that of a medical doctor. The realistic position for a PA or nurse practitioner is as a member of a physician's group, under the supervision of a medical doctor. Sending them out on their own into the community without reasonable physician supervision would be concerning. I am amazed that the powers in medicine would even consider sending PAs or nurse practitioners, with their limited medical training, into solo practice. Yet, at the same time, they make it mandatory that foreign-trained doctors—with far greater medical education training, post-medical-school training, and private clinical experience—repeat three years of residency before they can go into practice.

Still, it is definitely a reasonable plan to expand the total number of physician assistants or nurse practitioners in the field of primary care. Rapidly expanding PA or nurse practitioner programs would bring a significant number of new providers into the healthcare arena, in less than half the time it would take to train an MD. Again, this plan is only reasonable if the PA or nurse practitioner will be under the supervision of an MD.

Another innovative approach would be to recruit foreign-trained physicians who completed medical school abroad and have been practicing primary care for at least three years in their country of origin and bring them to the U.S. and enroll them in a comprehensive clinical program, similar to residency, where they would receive six months of U.S. clinical training, under the supervision of a medical doctor. Upon completing those six months, they would be licensed as physician assistants so they could work in the arena of primary care under the direct supervision of a licensed U.S. doctor.

It would be a challenge to say that a U.S.-trained physician assistant or nurse practitioner, with an average of three years of medical education, would be a higher quality provider or better-trained provider than a foreign-trained medical doctor who has also practiced medicine for three years. Foreign-trained doctors who would not want to become PAs would still have the option to complete three years of residency to become licensed physicians in the U.S. This is both a reasonable and controlled way to increase the number of primary-care providers in U.S. healthcare in a short period.

Since language and communication issues are a concern with some foreign doctors, they would all be required to take an English proficiency examination. An additional bonus to bringing in foreign-trained physicians as PAs is that there is no additional cost of training to get these individuals up to speed, thus saving the U.S. taxpayers' money. A foreign-trained physician costs the U.S. government about $100,000 a year for residency training. In this new model, the physician would pay, let's say, $20,000 for the six months of clinical training to become a PA. Instead of costing the government $100 million a year to train 1,000 foreign-trained doctors in residency, those doctors would pay the hospitals and medical staff that participate in the program $20 million for the six months of training.

The only question is whether the medical education governing bodies will explore all the presented options to fend off the pending physician shortage. If given the choice of battling Big Tobacco, the NRA, or the medical education governing bodies, I'll take my chances with Big Tobacco and the NRA combined. The fight would be less bloody.

# CHAPTER X
# PRIMARY CARE AND MINORITY PHYSICIANS
## We Need Help—Today

When I was a young boy, I, like many others, wanted to become a physician. If asked why, I'd respond that it was because I wanted to help people. I remember reading a story about a doctor by the name of Daniel Hale Williams who performed the first successful open-heart procedure. He happened to be African American. I made up my mind then that I would be a cardiologist.

Later in life, when I entered medical school, I intended to fulfill my goal of going into cardiology. As I rotated through different specialties, though, I found I really enjoyed family practice. It is not that I didn't enjoy cardiology anymore. The mission of the Morehouse School of Medicine, my alma mater, is to train physicians for and encourage physicians to pursue a career in primary care.

I chose family medicine over internal medicine or cardiology because of the versatility of the practice. I could see adults, I could see children, I could do deliveries, I could do minor surgical procedures, and I could do hospital work. For me, family medicine served the greater needs of the community. Family medicine is also considered the warm-and-fuzzy specialty. The family doctor in many communities was the country doc of old—the person the entire community came to whenever they had a medical issue, the doctor who didn't mind if you paid your bill in money or chickens. The way modern insurance reimbursements to physicians are cut to the bone, I am more inclined to take the chicken.

I enjoy being a family practitioner. More family doctors may be the key to our healthcare future. A well-trained family physician who can handle multiple medical problems means less referrals to specialists that are more expensive. Less referrals also mean less procedures performed, which ultimately means less overall medical costs. Unfortunately most medical school seniors are choosing not to go into family practice. One reason is the low level of reimbursement when compared to other specialties.

Family practice usually ranks somewhere near the bottom in physician reimbursement but at the top in total overhead expenses. Who would willingly choose that business model? Another more disheartening reason American senior medical students are choosing to go into specialties other than family medicine is that their medical school actively discourages them from the discipline. Medical schools routinely encourage their better academic students—their students with high board scores—to go into specialized medicine and stay away from family practice. The implication is that an academically strong student is too good for family practice.

All graduating medical school seniors go through the residency "match" process. This is a process whereby students apply to various medical specialty residency programs. During the 2006 match process, in the "core" specialties (internal medicine, family practice, OB-GYN, surgery, pediatrics and psychiatry) there were more applicants than available positions for every single one *except family practice.*

Family-practice residency directors scramble each year to find eligible students for their programs. There is an abundance of family-practice positions available despite the fact that over the last ten years there has been a steady decline in the number of family-practice residency positions. Today several family-practice programs struggle to keep their doors open. Continued low reimbursement and discouragement by the medical schools of careers in primary care will only signal a greater decline in family medicine in the future.

America is experiencing a decline in the specialty of family medicine at the very time there will be a greater need for family physicians as baby boomers enter their senior years. Family-practice docs are also the doctors who are more likely to practice in underserved areas such as inner cities and rural areas, compared to specialists. Of all the specialties, the perception for most is that family practice is the blue-collar specialty of medicine. And as blue-collar workers, we just do our jobs. We don't complain and we take everything and everyone one day at a time.

Studies show that international medical graduates are more willing than U.S. medical graduates to go into the specialty of family practice and practice in underserved rural and intercity communities. This is another reason international medical graduates, who require U.S. clinical experience before applying to residency, must be given an opportunity for training at U.S. hospitals.

Studies have been undertaken to assess the quality and value of primary-care physicians. One such study recently conducted by Dartmouth University indicates that states that have more general practitioners demonstrate a greater quality of care overall and have a lower cost per insured patient. This study also indicated that states with more specialists reported a lower quality of care overall and had a higher cost per insured patient.[28]

Solutions have to be created that will encourage medical students toward the specialty of family medicine. There needs to be better claims reimbursement, thereby increasing the total revenue generated by primary-care practices. The government might consider paying bonuses to graduate family-practice residents. Student loan debt relief is another option. Now is the time for governing bodies to act to reverse the downward spiral of U.S. medical students who choose specialties other than primary care.

Access to primary care is also critical to reverse the disproportionate rates of increased morbidity and mortality rates among minorities, particularly African American groups, in almost every disease category. African American women have higher infant mortality rates, 13.60 deaths per 1,000 live births (CDC 2004 report), compared to white women, 5.66 deaths per 1,000 live births (CDC 2004 report). A comparison of the U.S. infant mortality rate compared to other industrialized nations is the statistics experts like to routinely trot out as evidence of the breakdown of the U.S. healthcare system.

The U.S. spends more money per capita on healthcare, yet there are thirty plus nations with lower infant mortality rates. African Americans, Hispanics, Native Americans, and Asian/Pacific Islanders have higher infant mortality rates, lower life expectancy rates, and higher rates of cancer and cardiovascular disease than whites.[29] Here is an eye-opening statistic: although Latino Americans and African Americans make up greater than 25 percent of the population, they only comprise 6 percent of all physicians in America.[30] Asian Americans comprise 6 percent of the population but 16 percent of all physicians.[30] The lack of African American and Latino American physicians is particularly alarming since recent studies have shown that at times majority physicians unintentionally may not be as attentive to the dynamics and cultures of minority communities.[31]

Medicine is not just the objective evaluation of a patient's medical condition; it is also about subjective evaluation of a patient's social condition. One can prescribe all the drugs in the world, but if a patient cannot afford to purchase the drugs, there is a problem. If you tell the patient to come back for a critical procedure but the patient has no transportation, there is a problem.

Whether it's right or wrong, my experience is that minority patients feel more comfortable with physicians who look like them in the same way a significant proportion of women patients feel more comfortable with women doctors. The comfort I refer to is not about feeling a lack of competence or mistrust in the quality of medicine provided by majority physicians when they see minority patients. Some patients feel that when someone looks like them, that person understands what their lives are all about, without them having to explain it. Dr. Edith Fresh at Morehouse School of Medicine has lectured extensively on this issue of "cultural competency." We must address the disproportion of minority physician representation. There needs to be a greater effort to encourage young African American and Latino students to pursue a career in medicine.

There are two major obstacles facing these minority groups' acceptance to medical school. The first, as discussed earlier, is the limited availability of first-year medical school positions compared to the number of applicants. For more minority students to gain acceptance to medical school, it might mean denying admission to qualified nonminority students, and that would not be fair. The second obstacle is the historically lower GPAs and MCAT scores of African Americans and Latinos applicants.

GPA and MCAT scores are two heavily weighted factors used by medical school admissions committees. Lower scores do not always represent less academic intellect but, in many cases, less preparedness. Several factors—including a lack of minority role models or mentors in medicine, a lack of funds to take formal MCAT review courses, and a lack of proper guidance counseling through the college years—directly contribute to and are often the cause of this lack of preparedness.

Under the old scoring system, I never broke 1,000 on my SATs. When the other kids in my high school were going to SAT review classes on Saturday, I was watching television. I knew nothing about SAT review. My father knew even less than I did about properly preparing for college. When told I had to take the SATs, I just showed up, and my scores reflected my lack of preparation.

I went to Syracuse University after high school. When sitting in classes, head to head with my peers, in three of my first four semesters, my GPAs were 3.58, 3.33, and 3.81. When given a seat at the table, I performed. In college I had no clue how prepare for medical school. This may sound ridiculous, but I didn't even know what credits were. My roommate and some of the guys in my dorm helped me choose the classes for my freshman year. I had a better idea of what I was doing my sophomore year. It wasn't until my senior year that I began to look at the medical school application process, only to find out that I should have taken the MCAT at the end of my junior year. My opportunity to go to medical school directly after college was over. I had started too late in the game.

Things would have been different for me if I'd had a physician mentor through college. The first time I met and shook the hand of a black physician, I was twenty-two years old. I was a drug rep at the time and there were a handful of black physicians in my territory. When I had to choose a doctor, I chose Dr. James Hammond in Florence South Carolina, an African American. I chose him for two reasons: I felt he understood me, and he was glad to see a young black male succeeding in corporate America; I felt encouraged. I am not saying that blacks have to see blacks and whites have to see whites. I'm saying white physicians are ubiquitous, while black physicians are sparse. When African Americans see a like face in the exam room, a smile shines through.

It would be six years before I eventually started my medical school matriculation. In fact, I made up my mind that I was not going to go to medical school. I was a pharmaceutical rep in Atlanta, married and comfortable. It was only because of a friendship I developed with a medical professor at Morehouse School of Medicine, Dr. Peter Singleton, who encouraged me to apply to Morehouse, that I am a doctor today. This is the power of mentorship.

The limited number of bilingual Spanish- and English-speaking physicians will become more and more of a problem as the Spanish-speaking segment of the population continues to grow. If one is an African American who has historically not accessed the U.S. healthcare system but finds himself in an emergency room suffering with chest pain, at least he can communicate in English with healthcare providers regarding his symptoms, history, and any other pertinent information. If you are Latino, do not speak English, have not accessed the U.S. healthcare system, and arrive in the emergency room with chest pain, communication between you and your provider is a frustrating problem for both.

Lack of proper communication can easily lead to one of two situations: either misdiagnosis or the ordering of unnecessary tests and procedures as the doctors try to cover all the bases. Neither situation benefits the patient or the taxpayers. Hospitals and clinics try to use telephone services for translation help. Sometimes the children of the patients are asked to translate. Even with this go-between, there is increased risk of morbidity and mortality due to misinformation or miscommunication. Considering that Latinos are the largest minority group in America, this problem will only get worse.

There are opportunities to improve the number of physicians in primary care in the Latino American community. In my travels to Central and South America, I have found several reputable accredited medical school programs that would rival those found in the U.S. In some cases these programs produce more doctors than are needed in the community, especially in primary care. The cost of medical education in South America is also much less than in the U.S.

Given the fact that these programs overproduce physicians and the U.S. system currently under-produces physicians for residency programs, especially in the area of primary care, I see a great opportunity. We should collaborate with these South American schools to train Americans who qualify for U.S. medical school but are denied admission because of limited space. The cost of training one student in medicine in South America would be one-forth the U.S. cost. The additional U.S. dollars for these schools would allow them to expand and train even more local citizens in medicine.

The fact that Americans who train in South America would learn Spanish during their education would be an additional bonus. A physician who speaks Spanish would now have verbal access to a new and large patient population. We should also recruit physicians from countries that produce an excess number of physicians compared to the population. These physicians would be excellent candidates for U.S. primary-care residency programs. Foreign doctors who desire permanent U.S. residency after training would be obligated to serve in underserved Latino communities for a four-year period. This solution would show immediate results. Getting the program started is simply a matter of diplomacy and effort.

For African Americans, Latino Americans, or any student that does not get into U.S. medical schools, there are alternatives. Instead of an MD program, one may choose a DO (doctor of osteopathic medicine) program. DOs tend to have more training in manipulative therapy. One may choose to become a physician assistant (PA) or nurse practitioner. As mentioned earlier, nurse practitioners and PAs usually work under the supervision of an MD or DO. Another option for students who did not get into U.S. medical schools is to seek out a quality, offshore, U.S.-based-curriculum medical school program in the Caribbean. Thorough research is needed to ensure the Caribbean program is reputable.

All options have to be on the table for discussion to increase the number of primary-care physicians or providers in this country. All options have to be on the table for increasing the number of minority physicians in this country. Addressing these two issues may be a part of the solutions toward reversing the negative mortality disease trends in minority populations.

## CHAPTER XI
# EVERYONE HAS A RIGHT TO PROPER HEALTHCARE
## People Are People

What value can one put on health? How much would you pay for a cure if you had lung cancer? How much would you pay if your child needed a transplant? Would you exhaust your savings? Would you sell your house? Would you ask everyone you knew for money? If it meant living right above the poverty line, but you were cured or your child got the transplant, would it have been worth it to lose everything?

We spend so much time protecting our possessions. We spend so much time squirreling away our nuts to prepare for retirement. What does any of it matter if you or your child dies in six months? I, like you, don't even like to think about those things.

When the republican white house press secretary, Tony Snow, announced his cancer had returned a week after the wife of the democratic presidential candidate John Edwards announced her cancer had returned, who cared about their politics, except Rush Limbaugh? When cancer hits a family, it is like throwing a brick through their window of life; all is shattered. Everyone involved cries. Everyone cries a lot, eventually.

I didn't cry at age fourteen, when my mother told us she had colon cancer. I was in denial. I didn't cry during the funeral. I kept looking forward, at the pastor and at the casket. At the end of the service, I turned around to walk behind the casket and I saw the look on everyone's face. For some there was the look of crushing grief. For some there was the look of pity. That was the first time I really understood that my mother was dead. She was not coming back. I hadn't seen that on her face earlier at the funeral home as I quickly glanced at her. I saw it now on the faces of the living who were mourning my mother. I went home and cried for a long time that night.

No one today in America should die of colon cancer. No one today in America should die of breast cancer. No one today in America should die of prostate cancer. No one in today America should die of cervical cancer. No one in today America should die of ovarian cancer. We are spending a lot of time and money looking for cures we already have for most cancers. The cure is prevention. The cure is screening. Screening works.

Because of my mother's death from colon cancer, I underwent the colon cancer screening at age thirty-seven. The recommended colonoscopy screening for colon cancer is at age fifty, unless you have a family member die of colon cancer before age fifty, and then you are tested earlier. They found two polyps during my procedure. Who knows what my situation would be in the future if I had not gotten the colonoscopy. The procedure is safe, painless, and quick. Everyone over the age of fifty in America should have a colonoscopy, unless of course, one is uninsured and cannot afford it. A significant number of people, who aren't screened, for whatever reason, will die. One hundred thousand people a year die of this preventable disease. Why?

There are two types of heart-wrenching pain, depression, and terror of the unknown: (1) the pain, depression, and terror of the unknown test result that may indicate our loved one may be gravely sick and (2) the pain, depression, and terror of the unknown test result that may indicate that you are gravely ill. I have been through both, with the premature deaths of my parents and twice personally.

About two years ago, I applied for disability insurance. The results of one of my blood tests was elevated. The test was repeated and the results were again higher than normal. Something, somewhere, was going on in my bones. I was denied the insurance. Go figure. I did what many people do: I cursed the insurance company and blew it off. I felt healthy and the test was nonspecific. I ran it by some of my colleagues and they didn't seem to think it was anything. A year later I tried again to get disability insurance and I was denied again because of the same high reading. I still felt fine.

This time I decided I would get a full workup to prove to the insurance company that nothing was wrong with me. I did a bone scan. The radiology tech prepped me and put me on the table. I nodded off during the procedure. When I opened my eyes, the radiology tech and now the radiologist were looking at me with a worried look on their faces. I immediately asked, "What's wrong?" The radiologist said there was a spot on my left pelvis what was concerning. They wanted to repeat the study and pay close attention to my pelvis. This time I was fully awake for the procedure. My first thought was that it was probably just an artifact or something benign, and nothing to worry about. When the scan got to my hips, my left pelvis lit up on the monitor in front of me like a Christmas tree. A cold sweat washed over me. I was now thinking the worst. This to me was malignancy. I jumped off the table went to the radiologist and asked for his opinion. He said, "I don't know. We need other studies."

I got home that night. I didn't say anything to my family. I didn't want to alarm them if nothing was really wrong. I guess I could have gone the other way and involved them from the beginning, but I chose not to. I reviewed studies and textbooks and searched the internet. Everything to me was leaning toward deadly osteosarcoma.

I reflected back to the first time I was faced with the possibility of a life-ending illness, the time I got shingles in residency and every symptom pointed toward HIV. I avoided a bullet then when my HIV test was negative. I avoided a bullet when my colon polyps were benign. I had been through so much already regarding my health. I had gone through so much with the illnesses of my parents. Why me again? I was depressed and I was angry. Why was God doing this to me again? I was a Christian. Why me again? I tried to bargain with God. "Lord, please let this cup pass before me." I then asked God to grant me a sense of peace, no matter what the results of the follow-up test revealed.

I got an MRI the next day to clarify the diagnosis. I not only got the MRI but a CT scan and plain films as well. I underwent more tests in twenty-four hours than most people could get in two weeks. I had the films read by radiology, endocrinology, and orthopedics. Thank the Lord the diagnosis was not a malignant bone cancer; it was Paget's disease, a disease common in old Jewish Mediterranean men. I wasn't old and I wasn't Jewish. Whatever the case, I didn't have bone cancer, and the Lord chose to spare me again. As a side note, the insurance company still turned me down for disability. I was lucky, but not everyone gets good news about test results. Even if my news was bad, I at least had health insurance for treatment.

Throughout all my health scares, at least I had good health insurance. The tests I completed regarding my Paget's would have costs thousands of dollars if I'd had to pay for them myself. If the tests were positive for malignancy, it would have cost tens of thousands out of pocket to treat. At least I had health insurance. What does the person who does not have health insurance do if they are faced with the same health issues I faced and their test results come back positive for malignancy?

I have had many conversations with people about the tremendous number of uninsured in America. Many believe the uninsured are lazy individuals that do not want to work and only want to live off others' tax dollars. Granted, some people fit that description, but that is not the case for the majority. Most of the uninsured are working Americans, employed by small business owners that cannot provide health insurance.

They are your barbers and your beauticians. They are your cleaners and your convenience store workers. They are your landscapers and your house painters. They are your childcare workers and your church support staff. They are several people that live on your block, down the road, or in your subdivision. They are your neighbors and the children of your neighbors.

They are your family of four without a preexisting illness, that cannot foot the bill of one thousand dollars per month for basic health insurance. They are your family of four in which Mom has diabetes and one of the children has asthma, and because of the preexisting conditions they are looking at possibly two thousand dollars per month for health insurance. They are your family of four that pray every night for a job with health benefits. They are your family of four that see their small life savings wiped out by one unexpected health mishap. They are your family of four that get strange looks at the doctor's office when they state they do not have health coverage.

What family of four am I talking about? The next time you drive home, count houses. Living in every sixth house is that family of four to whom I refer. Are we our brothers' keepers? You're darn right we are. We had better be, because one day we may be the ones living in that sixth house on the block.

It's not that Americans are not generous with each other and with those overseas. No one out-gives Americans after a disaster. Whether Hurricane Katrina on our soil or a tsunami in the Pacific, we give. We give a lot. But why must we wait for a disaster to give? Why do we have to wait to see the suffering first? Is the prospect of volumes of death not real unless CNN or FoxNews covers it?

Almost two thousand people died in Katrina. More than three thousand died on 9/11. There are 47 million uninsured Americans. This year as many as 18,000 of them will die for reasons associated with being uninsured. Next year another 18,000 will die. The following year another 18,000 will die. How many times do I have to write this? What will it take for all of America to get involved with this issue? There is no greater issue facing this America today than healthcare.

We spend $2 trillion a year on this issue. That number will double in five to eight years. Where is the money going to come from? You cannot put the burden on small business. They don't have the money. Big business doesn't have the money either. Just look at the automotive industry. Last year Detroit spent $12 billion on healthcare. Their competitors spent 10 percent of that. How can we compete? Individuals who seek policies have no buying power to command reasonable premiums from the insurance industry. Drugs prices are going through the roof. Why are we waiting to focus our full attention on these problems? What will it take to lock all the smart people in a room and not let them out until they have a solution?

America's biggest problem is that we can "afford" tragedy. We don't try to prevent disaster because we have the money to throw at the disaster after the fact. The government knew that if the levies in New Orleans were not reinforced, a break was inevitable, and the results would be tragic. The estimated cost of repair was about $4 billion. It did nothing. The levies broke; thousands of people died. Thousands more were displaced. The estimated cost of the aftermath is now more than $100 billion dollars.

We were warned, we did nothing, the levies broke; people died; we threw money at it after the fact. That was the sequence of events in the past. That is the sequence of events today, and I pray that will not be the sequence of events tomorrow regarding healthcare and the uninsured. By the way, a massive earthquake will strike Los Angeles. Is government addressing that proactively? Does the average Joe on the street have an evacuation plan for himself and his family? My guess would be no.

Jamaica went through a devastating hurricane about twenty years ago, Hurricane Gilbert. Jamaica had been through other storms but none as devastating as Gilbert turned out to be. Well, Jamaica is not a rich country and it couldn't afford another Gilbert. The Jamaicans couldn't stop future storms, but they could develop a thorough national hurricane plan as well as comprehensive evacuation and communication procedures. That is exactly what they did.

Poorer nations don't have the technology, access to care, drugs, hospital networks, and specialist expertise we have in America. They have to invest in prevention. We have all the money in the world, but we'll worry about disease after the fact. We had better wake up. We are in a global economy. Every nation has the U.S. in their crosshairs. America has all the money in the world today, but if we do not change our ways, maybe not tomorrow.

I always wondered why the government did not pay, prior to the new prescription drug benefit, for medication for the elderly. Cardiovascular disease kills 500,000 Americans each year. The risk factors for heart attack over age forty-five are hypertension, diabetes, hypercholesterolemia, family history of heart attack, and smoking. I would guess that the average American has several of these risk factors.

To prevent heart attack, generic medications would cost about one hundred dollars a month for a person with hypertension, diabetes, and hypercholesterolemia; the government was unwilling to pay for the medications. If that same person had a stroke or a heart attack, the government would pay the cost of hospitalization, intensive care, and rehabilitation, all of which can cost more than $250,000. The cost of $1,200 a year for pills and prevention versus $250,000 after the fact; the math seems clear on the surface.

If you analyze further you realize something: someone in government has done a different kind of math. Some number-cruncher realized that it would cost the government more to pay for the pills for all than to pay the cost of a few who stroked or had a heart attack. How tragic. Russian roulette with peoples lives. That is just not right. I knew some of those people who couldn't afford their medications and suffered a heart attack as a result.

I remember getting a call one night that one of my patients was in the hospital because she just had a heart attack. She was a senior. She had multiple medical problems. We juggled her medications as best we could. She had no health benefits other than Medicare, so she did not have any prescription drug benefits. She had coronary bypass surgery the next day. I went to the hospital to see her. I walked into to the cardiac ICU to see how she was doing. I asked the charge nurse for her. She told me that my patient had died during surgery. I stood there just staring into space for a few seconds. She apparently could not get off the bypass pump during the procedure and she passed away. Well, fortunately for the government, there would be no $250,000 tab for her rehab. She died.

I must seem like a far left-wing liberal to some right now, but I really am not. I am conservative on most other issues. I gladly served in the armed forces. I do not believe in government controlling our lives. I don't believe taxing Americans for everything under the sun is productive. But I do believe all Americans have basic rights. We have a right to protection by the government from all enemies, foreign and domestic. A giant enemy we face here in America today is the death of more than 18,000 people annually because of lack of healthcare coverage. All of those Americans have the basic right to live. Being fortunate enough to have a job that provides a healthcare benefit does not give one more of a right to live than someone who cannot afford insurance. Government has the obligation to protect those 47 million uninsured Americans. I am passionate about this issue because, as a physician, I see the difference between the haves and the have-nots on a regular basis.

It is hard for the layperson to understand the life-and-death decisions physicians have to face each day. Trying to treat patients with multiple medical problems and no money for medication is a serious problem. There are also other strains on physicians to make the right decisions or suggestions in the care of our patients. You try to make the best decisions you can. Sometimes you make recommendations with horrible results.

There was a pleasant lady I saw on a regular basis. She had coronary artery disease; the arteries of her heart had blockages in their lumen. Cardio-thoracic surgery recommended a heart bypass. This is a procedure during which the blocked arteries that supplied blood to her heart would be essentially replaced or bypassed. She asked me for my opinion.

I told her that if she chose to do the bypass she would have more energy and she wouldn't be as fatigued, something of which she always complained. I told her that if she didn't have the surgery she risked having a heart attack. I told her that if she were my mother I would recommend she have the procedure. She said she was scared and maybe she could live with the fatigue. I encouraged her again to have the bypass surgery, and she reluctantly agreed. I was very happy she agreed to do the procedure. She was going to do fine. She would rehab well and thank me for making her feel better.

I was there when she came out of surgery. She was intubated, on a breathing machine, which was normal. A couple of days went by and she was still on the ventilator. I spoke with pulmonary about the situation. They told me that because she was a smoker she would take longer to get off the ventilator. I told her the situation. I encouraged her to stay strong.

Days went by and she was still on the vent. A week after the procedure, she was still no closer to having the breathing tube down her throat removed. Then the bad news came: pulmonary told me that her lungs were in worse shape than they thought and it was unlikely that she would come off the ventilator any time soon, if at all. She would be sent from ICU to a long-term respiratory-failure care facility.

This was a woman who was used to being out and about. Now she was bedridden and on a ventilator because of respiratory failure. I blamed myself. The pulmonologist had already broken the news to my patient. It was so hard for me to walk into that ICU room and face her, but I did. I walked in. I looked at her. Tears started rolling down her face. I spent a little time with her. I tried to encourage her to stay strong. I walked out. I was crushed.

She was transferred to the long-term care facility. I never saw her again. I made a few calls to the medical staff at the facility to inquire about her progress. I got the standard answer, "She's fine." I never visited her. I couldn't. I felt guilty. I thought she definitely blamed me for her fate. A few months later, I told an older doctor and a friend what happened and how I blamed myself. Dr Jenkins told me something I never will forget. He said, "As physicians, sometimes we get bad outcomes from making the right decisions. Right decisions do not guarantee good results." He was absolutely right. I felt better.

I have done other things out of the ordinary to help uninsured patients in need. It's been almost ten years since I did the next thing I want to disclose to help an uninsured patient. I assume any statute of limitations has now expired. When I was a resident completing my internal medicine rotation, I had a patient who had a previous history of heart disease, and it appeared that he had another mild heart attack. He was a truck driver. He had some "wife separation" issues, he was between jobs, and he had just gotten into town to look for a job.

He started having chest pain and he was subsequently admitted to a hospital that treated uninsured patients. Tests results indicated that he did suffer another mild heart attack. After a few days, he improved and it was time for his discharge. He had no money; he had no place to go. He seemed like an all right guy who was just in a bad situation. I went to the ATM downstairs in the hospital and withdrew some money for him.

I was very familiar with his situation. Years earlier I had been having serious financial problems. The problem was very easy to define. I had a lot more monthly debt than income. Several members from my church each gave me fifty dollars a month to pay my mortgage. I never had to ask for it. Every month they tracked me down and gave me the money. I was very appreciative of their kindness. I wanted to help my patient financially if I could. I extended the money to him. He hesitated. I could see he was a little embarrassed. I told him it was okay; when I was in need, people helped me. He reluctantly took the money and was very thankful.

There was still the issue of housing. I gave him a pair of hospital scrubs and a key to one of the resident call rooms. For about a week, he just blended in with everyone else at the hospital. He later got a room at the YMCA. He eventually got back on his feet. He got a job and became a productive citizen again. I believe his situation was indicative of that of millions of Americans who encounter the double whammy of financial hardship coupled with serious health issues. Everyone without health insurance literally could lose everything they own to pay their medical bills after a heart attack or a stroke or cancer. To make matters worse, hospitals routinely charge the uninsured more than the insured for the same procedures. Talk about piling it on.

All physicians—whether white, black, Latino, or Asian—should be sensitive to the social symptoms, such as a lack of insurance, as well as the physical symptoms of our patients. The average physician's notes consists of a great deal of objective data but very little subjective social concern; we need a balance of both to truly meet the needs of a significant proportion of our society.

When I was in residency, after call, I would always have to present to the other residents and attending physicians what patients I admitted the night before. One attending in particular, Dr. Jones, would always spend three times more time on the social issues of my patients. Normally we blew through that section. If, however, you were going to be presenting to Dr. Jones, you had better know everything about the social life of your patient.

I still use that practice today. The patient population in one of my practices is 90 percent black, indigent Medicare/Medicaid, and democrat. The patient population in my other practice is 90 percent Caucasian, middle and upper class, well insured, and Republican. One patient introduced himself as "the only democrat in town." My medical knowledge is no greater than that of the average primary-care provider. My success in both practices has come because of the additional time I spend on social concerns that face all my patients—black, white, rich, poor, democrat or republican. Taking care of a patient's hypertension or high cholesterol is appreciated far less than asking them about their son's last softball game. I think Dr. Jones would be proud of me.

The issues of the uninsured are close to me because I was in the same boat twelve years ago. I had very little money. I had no insurance for my family or me. My wife actually got milk vouchers for my baby girl. I really do not like thinking about those times, but thank God I was not in that position for very long. No one got seriously ill, and there were people around me to help. But what about people who find themselves in the position I was in for more than a few months? What about people who find themselves without health insurance for years—

people with "preexisting medical conditions" who may never qualify for or be able to afford health insurance?

It has taken me two years to write this book. I wrote portions of it on four continents and in more than six countries. On my trips I watched people. I saw them come and go. I saw them laugh and cry. Whether in Kuala Lampur; Malaysia; Bogota Columbia; Amsterdam, Netherlands; Vancouver, British Columbia; Flint, Michigan; or New Orleans, Louisiana, people are people. Not one life is more or less valuable than another. Everyone, if given the choice, wants to live.

Can the powers that be find a way to prevent the death of another 18,000 uninsured Americans this year or next? Is it important enough to them?

Remember, in every sixth house on your block lives an uninsured family. There are 47 million uninsured Americans who still fall through the cracks in this country. We have to do better. We may not pay now, but we will pay later. We always do. Am I my brother's keeper? The answer for me is yes. What is your answer?

# CHAPTER XII

# THE BENNETT PLAN FOR THE U.S. HEALTHCARE SYSTEM
## Politics, Power Brokers, Prevention, Preparation, and Partnership

First let's get one proposed solution out of the way: government-regulated universal healthcare like Canada. Forget it. That system will not work in America for many reasons. I'll discuss the most important one. America is a "right now" society for everything. We don't wait for anything. Not only do we not wait; we become indignant when we are forced to wait. I have seen people go ballistic waiting for a latte. The Canadian healthcare system is all about waiting.

I am sorry; I'm over forty and if I have chest pain, I want to get worked up today to ensure I am not having a heart attack. I do not want to wait to see a cardiologist. I do not want to wait to get a stress test. I do not want to wait to get a cardiac catherization. I certainly will not wait in line until it's my turn to get bypass surgery.

I was flying to Toronto a few months ago and I struck up a conversation about the Canadian healthcare system with the passenger sitting next to me. He was in the U.S. as a Canadian electrical contactor in New Orleans. He hurt his knee while on the job and was flying home to see an orthopedic surgeon. I thought the injury was a recent occurrence, but he told me he hurt himself six months ago. I said six month is a long time to wait to see if you had an ACL injury. He said it really should not have taken six months. It should have taken three months to see the specialist, but when he flew back to Canada three months earlier, the surgeon was on vacation, so they rescheduled him another three months. Three months is long enough to wait to see an orthopedic surgeon. Six months is ridiculous. Can you imagine the level of anxiety you would suffer if you knew you needed cardiac bypass surgery and would have to wait a couple of months? No American would accept that. Actually, there is a group of Americans who would love this system. They're called lawyers.

Another reason the Canadian system won't work here is that 47 million Americans do not have healthcare coverage. That's 10 million more people than the entire population of Canada; which is about one-tenth that of the U.S. Ten times larger means ten times more headache. This reminds me of the debate in 1992 between Governor Bill Clinton of Arkansas, President George Bush, and Ross Perot. Perot was addressing Bill Clinton's "lack of experience." Someone reminded Perot that Clinton was the governor of Arkansas. Perot's response was that just because someone can run a general store doesn't mean you give them the keys to Wal-Mart. Canada: the general store, America: Wal-Mart. I must concede, though, that the general-store fella for many was a very effective president. What are some things to consider to reform our healthcare system?

## POLITICS

I have long given up the notion that changes in the healthcare system will come about because of compassion for our fellow man. It is sad to say that the only thing that really drives change regarding any situation in this country revolves around two areas: number one is money, number two is politics. On the other hand, maybe number one is politics and number two is money. Either way, if we are going to look for solutions to the dilemmas that were presented in prior chapters, those solutions will have to incorporate either a profit motive or political motive.

The first thing we have to do is make sure we have the right team that has our agenda in mind—the team that will carry the ball on these pertinent issues. That team starts with the politicians who set the policy and the agenda in Congress. I am not one to usually express myself by using vulgarity, but I can find no other phrase to sum up how I believe the typical politician feels about healthcare and the problems of healthcare in this country than the phrase "they don't give a damn." "Healthcare for all" or "We need to do better in healthcare" are campaign slogans for most politicians; I do not know if there is commitment there.

You can also forget about politicians cutting wasteful spending in other areas to free up funds to improve healthcare. Remember, one man's pork is another man's dinner. I vote for your dinner today and you vote for my dinner tomorrow, wink, wink. Pork gets politicians reelected to office. In general it is safe to say that most politicians are motivated by whatever issues allow them to stay in office. If the issues do not matter in polling, the issues do not matter to them. That's fine. As individuals concerned about healthcare, we need to know the political motivation factors and work those factors to our advantage.

Most polls will show that many Americans put healthcare in the top three areas of concern, the economy and the war being the other two. But while the situation in Iraq has forced politicians to take a stance for or against, there has been no such definitive stance for politicians in regard to the issue of global healthcare for all Americans. They all talk a good game, but are they committed?

Here then is the first step toward finding a solution and getting the team together. If you are an uninsured American, if you see no prayer of ever getting healthcare from your employer, if you are concerned about yourself or your loved ones getting sick and wiping out your life savings, you need to make just a few telephone calls.

I have enclosed in the last chapters of this book the names, addresses, phone and fax numbers of the 110th Congress House of Representatives and Senate. First call the local office of your local U.S. congressperson. Let the person who answers the phone know that you are a member of the congressperson's district. Ask to speak directly with your congressperson. If you are unable to speak with them directly, then ask to set up a meeting with your local congressperson. Their representative will continue to do a tap dance on the telephone, trying to appease you in an attempt to avoid letting you speak directly with your congressperson. Try your best, though, to get that appointment or phone conversation. Be a little pushy if you have to; don't be nasty, just a little pushy. You may have to make more than one telephone call. You may have to personally go down to the office. But if you really care about securing healthcare, you have to make the effort. Once you are able to speak directly with your local congressperson via a telephone call or in person, tell them the following: "I am an uninsured American. Will you actively support legislation that ensures that I will have an opportunity to secure affordable healthcare coverage for myself and my family?"

After the first dodge to avoid answering the question by your congressperson, repeat the question: "I am an uninsured American. Will you actively support legislation that ensures that I will have an opportunity to secure affordable healthcare coverage for myself and my family?" If you cannot get a clear yes to that question, it's time to consider voting for the other guy.

Let me make this clear: if you are uninsured, there is zero chance of you being insured without the intervention of Congress. Making a few phone calls or taking a trip to your congressperson's office is not an unreasonable step if it gives you and your family a shot of getting healthcare coverage. If you get a yes, you vote for him or her. But, if you get a no or a response that is a little bit foggy—a little bit unclear—and you are not certain if the response was a yes or no, you need to go visit the opposition and pose the same question.

If the opposition's answer seems a little bit foggy, just like your current congressperson's answer seemed a little bit foggy, vote for the opposition anyway. Why vote for the other guy? You need to send a clear message to your local congressperson that if they are unwilling to support you on the agenda of insuring you have proper healthcare coverage, you will take your chances with someone else.

Once you have accomplished that task with your congressperson, the next step is to call one of your U.S. senators. Ask to speak directly to your U.S. senator. There will be a tap dance here again: "Can I help you? Can someone else here in the office help you?" Your answer will be no. You want to speak directly with your senator. If you are not getting through by telephone, then go down to the office and ask to speak with your senator. Here again be a little pushy of you have to. Don't be nasty, just a little pushy.

Once you meet with your senator or have your senator on the telephone, ask the following question: "I am an uninsured American. Will you actively support legislation that ensures I will have the opportunity to secure affordable healthcare coverage for myself and my family?" If you get a fuzzy response, repeat the question. Again, if you do not get a clear yes or an answer that you are very comfortable with—if you get a foggy answer, if you get an outright no—call the person running against your senator and ask the same question. If the answer is yes, fine. If the answer is cloudy or confusing, fine. Vote for the other guy. Repeat this practice with your next U.S. senator.

What if you're not in a district or state where your congressperson is not up for reelection in the next cycle? That is okay. Ask the questions and get an answer. At least you know where the people who represent you in government stand. Call all the representatives in your state if you can, and ask the question. The important thing to remember here is you are not doing this by yourself. You have 47 million friends. You have to know that you are not alone; you have to know that your effort will not be in vain. You need to inform and encourage uninsured individuals you know to perform the same exercise with their local Washington representatives.

If you cannot call, then fax or write a letter to your congressman and senators. Ask the question; "I am an uninsured American. Will you actively support legislation that ensures that I will have an opportunity to secure affordable healthcare coverage for myself and my family? If you do not get an answer in 30 days, then write or fax the question again. Keep repeating the task until you get an answer. This is your opportunity to empower yourself. You no longer have to be a victim. Turn to the section of this book where your representatives and senators are listed. Find your representatives and make the calls. This one issue and this one effort by uninsured Americans can literally decide the next president and the next Congress of the United States. Do your part.

We can talk about the war, we can talk about abortion, we can talk about immigration, we can talk about the economy, we can talk about gay and lesbian rights, we can talk about stem cell research, and we can talk about tax cuts. But for you, an uninsured American, there is no greater issue that affects your life—day in, day out—than the issue of not having healthcare insurance. Forget about all the other platforms. Forget about being a republican, forget about being a democrat, forget about being an independent, forget about being a libertarian, and forget about being a member of the green party. You need to vote for the presidential candidate who will actively support your agenda of securing affordable healthcare.

Without proper healthcare for you and your family, you are literally walking through a minefield every day. Without notice and without preparation, a healthcare tragedy can strike you or your family. What would your stance on the war matter or your stance on abortion matter then? What would your stance on the economy or your stance on stem cell research matter then? What would your opinion on taxes matter if severe illness strikes you or your family? Do not be swayed, do not be moved, do not compromise, do not bargain, and do not retreat! This is your issue for the next election. Make your voice heard. Once the politicians understand how serious we are; more importantly, how numerous you are; and *most* importantly, how willing we are to vote, they will have to act or lose their jobs.

**POWER BROKERS**

The billion-dollar question is, how do you bring 47 million people into the healthcare system and not break the bank? I stated earlier that there are two areas that have to be conquered to address the issue of the uninsured American. We addressed the politicians; now let's deal with economics.

Let's look at the numbers. In 2006 the total number of dollars spent on healthcare was approximately two trillion dollars. The breakdown is as follows: 47 percent to hospitals, 21 percent to physicians and physician-related services, 10 percent to pharmaceuticals, 10 percent to dental, and 10 percent to administration.[32] Assuming an insurance cost of two hundred dollars per month per uninsured individual, insuring 47 million individuals would cost approximately $9.4 billion per month, or $112 billion dollars annually. Two hundred dollars per month for medical insurance is a reasonable figure when you factor in healthy individuals, children, and individuals who may have some long-term chronic-disease issues. Now where are we going to get $112 billion dollars annually?

Should we tax everyone to pay for this? I doubt the majority of Americans are willing to choose this option, especially if the government will be administrating the program. The government has rarely, in my opinion, proved to be up to the task of managing much of anything, not necessary because of lack of effort. There are just too many levels of bureaucracy. Should we pull the funds from other budgets? Maybe twenty years from now Congress will agree where in the budget to get the money. Should this money come from wasteful spending and pork projects? Good luck with that one.

Should we mandate that all businesses provide health insurance for their employees? This would bankrupt small businesses that are already struggling to be profitable in this global economy. Currently U.S. businesses have to compete in a global economy where the healthcare of the employees of their worldwide competitors is subsidized by their government. Burdening all small business with healthcare for their employees, in my opinion, will lead to layoffs, decreased quality of goods, burnout, and decreased productivity as small companies extend kept employee work hours as a desperate measure to maintain productivity.

Should the government develop some sort of tax credit system for the uninsured? For that to work families would have to have the resources to pay for insurance and then look to get the benefit of the tax credit the following year. A family of five, with a net monthly income of three thousand dollars, would pay about one thousand dollars per month for health insurance, hoping to get a tax credit the following year. What happens if they are unable to keep up with their health insurance premiums? Does the family's health insurance lapse? Is there a penalty to pay? Wouldn't that be counterproductive?

Mandating healthcare insurance is often compared to mandated car insurance. Well not so fast. When it comes to car insurance one has options, (1) do not drive and instead take the bus or (2) drive a car one can afford to insure. Do not buy a Mercedes when you can only afford the insurance of a Mercury. When it comes to mandated health insurance, one cannot simply opt out of it like deciding not to drive, and the health insurance premium payments are closer to insurance payments of the Mercedes than the Mercury. Mandating health insurance is not the answer either.

So how do we find the $112 billion a year needed to allow uninsured Americans access to the healthcare system? We spoke about the politicians; now let us turn our attention to the power brokers. We must get the money from those who would profit most by bringing millions of people into the system. These groups combine to make the $2 trillion annually spent on healthcare. These are the power brokers:

hospitals, insurance companies, physicians, pharmaceutical companies, and other healthcare suppliers.

A 4.2 percent tax on gross revenue of the power brokers would raise approximately 75 percent of the $112 billion needed. If each uninsured individual contributed fifty dollars per month toward healthcare insurance, that would raise the other 25 percent. Now, before doctors, hospitals, insurance companies, and all the other entities that would be paying this contribution scream bloody murder, let me tell you why this plan is good for them.

First, it is clear to see why the insurance company would benefit from this plan. This plan brings $112 billion of revenue into their coffers. I believe market-driven insurance companies would do a better job than the federal government in the administration, monitoring, cost-containment, and quality-control aspects of this plan. Adding 47 million people to the healthcare system means a potential 15 percent increase of patients for doctors and hospitals, meaning more revenue. In any business a 4.2 percent investment that may mean a 15 percent increase in revenue would be a wise investment.

A solo practice grossing $300,000 a year in revenue would pay an additional tax of $12,600 but could see an additional $45,000 in revenue. Stark Laws that limit physician participation in certain medical revenue streams could be adjusted to help offset the tax on physicians. Hospitals would see a great increase in revenues from admissions, outpatient procedures, and diagnostics. A total of 47 million more people could now get prescription drugs, making the pharmaceutical companies more profitable.

With this plan an uninsured family of five would now pay $250 and not $1,000 per month for healthcare benefits, a reasonable burden.

The fifty dollar figure per family member per month for health care premiums could be adjusted upward based upon income for working uninsured families. Individuals who participate in this plan would have a benefit package similar to the base Kaiser Permanente plan; no frills and no bells and whistles. Although controversial, this model has proved to deliver quality care and control healthcare costs. I believe that all Americans are entitled to basic healthcare coverage for office visits, prescription drugs, diagnostics, surgery, home health, and hospitalization. Those who want more than the basics would have to generate the income to afford the upgrade. People who can only afford to live in $80,000 homes that provides shelter, heat, electricity, water, and security cannot demand to live in a $1 million home with upgrades. If people want the upgrades, they—not industry or the government via our tax dollars—should pay for them.

This healthcare model would stimulate a modest redistribution of physicians. Areas of the country that traditionally had high numbers of uninsured would now have paying patients. The market would drive physician redistribution, not compassion or guilt or government incentive plans. It is all about economics, not emotion.

## PREVENTION

Now that we have looked at getting people in political office who actually care about healthcare and we have looked at a plan to raise the funds necessary to bring the uninsured into the healthcare marketplace, let's look at ways of controlling future cost. It is estimated that the total dollars that would be spent in healthcare by 2017 would be about a $4 trillion, or double what is spent today. Those numbers cannot continue to grow at such an alarming rate.

We have the solution for slowing down the growth of this healthcare system right in front of us. It has always been in front of us. We also have a solution for the major cancers that develop and kill Americans annually. There is a solution to decreasing the billions of dollars spent on heart attacks and strokes annually. The trillion-dollar answer here is prevention. Prevention, prevention, and a third time, prevention—prevention via education and screening.

No one in this country should die of breast cancer, prostate cancer, colon cancer, cervical cancer, uterine cancer, or ovarian cancer. Those are all cancers that can be easily screened for today. But you cannot screen people who are not a part of the healthcare system or have limited knowledge of the healthcare system. This is where we bring in one of America's most effective tools, Madison Avenue. If I say the purple pill, something pops into the average individual's mind. If I say the blue pill, something else pops into the average person's mind. One thing the pharmaceutical industry has clearly shown the healthcare industry is that advertising drives consumer education and that means increased market share.

Screening for common cancers and steps to prevent heart disease and stroke have to be brought to the American public via a high-powered advertising campaign. Forget about a thirty-second boring public service announcement on health. Dynamic and innovative television and print ads about the issues of screening and prevention will make a difference. If solid advertising did not work, corporate America would not be using it so effectively. If we put approximately $300 million dollars a year into TV advertisement educating Americans about prevention and screenings, a significant number of dollars could be saved in healthcare expenditures.

Hypertension is a major risk factor for heart disease. It costs thirty dollars per month for blood pressure medication. It costs more than $250,000 to treat and rehab a heart attack victim. What would you rather spend? Advertisement would be centered around the three following areas: heart disease, cancer, and stroke—the big three.

Where should the $300 million dollars come from to pay for this advertising? First, we should solicit the major networks and cable stations to run the ads gratis in prime time. Second, the bulk of the dollars should come from the insurance and pharmaceutical industries. The insurance industry because prevention means fewer dollars paid out later for cure or treatment. The pharmaceutical industry for two reasons: the first being it has the money now and will have even more later once the windfall revenues (approximately $500 billion over the next ten years) from Medicare part D comes in; second, the pharmaceutical industry should also pay for these ads because more office visits means more prescriptions written. A total of $300 million dollars annually for healthcare promotion and prevention ads is a drop in the bucket for an industry that spends more than that annually for advertising just two drugs, Lipitor and Crestor.

## PREPARATION

Let's move on to another area in healthcare that could save billions, the area of preparation. That is the issue of advanced directives. It should be mandatory that all Americans have advanced directives. What are advanced directives? They are instructions to healthcare providers regarding what you want done if you find yourself in a position where you are unable to make medical decisions, for instance, if you were in a coma. You make your wishes known on paper, or to a loved one, regarding shock treatment to revive you if your heart stops or putting you on a breathing machine if your lungs stop.

This is information that, in my opinion, should be collected by all healthcare insurance companies at the point of registration and renewed annually. I have seen many cases where individuals suffer massive trauma or heart attack or stroke and have virtually zero chance of recovery to even a minimal standard of quality of life. The patient invariably has no advanced directive, so it is now left to their loved ones to make hard decisions. That puts a tremendous burden on the loved one who is already devastated by the tragedy before them.

If your husband, your wife, your mother, or your father was in a terrible accident or had a heart attack or a stroke and had a 0.001 percent chance of recovery after intense resuscitation attempts, tubes, blood and fluids going in and out every orifice, what would you chose to do? Would you say, "No, don't do anything, just make them comfortable?" or would you say "Do everything you can"?

It really shouldn't be about what *you* want to do; it should be about what you believe the person who suffered the trauma would want for themselves. When advanced directives do not exist, no one wants to be in the position of saying "Just make my loved one comfortable, do nothing." There is real fear, especially in some cultures, that if you agree to stop life support, you agree to kill your loved one. The person with a .001 percent chance of recovery may be your spouse and you just eliminated even that small possibility by agreeing to stop life support. Could you live with the guilt of not giving your loved one a minimal opportunity of survival–even if it meant that the best you could hope for is that they remain on a ventilator, brain dead for the rest of their life?

Advanced directives would lift the burden from a family member if tragedy struck a loved one; for me that is the primary benefit of advanced directives: to prevent the guilt. The secondary benefit is the economics. Take the case where there was a terminally ill patient in the ICU. This patient had acute pancreatitis. An assessment of his condition indicated a 100 percent mortality picture, meaning there was a 100 percent likelihood the patient was going to die. The patient coded. We revived him, but he coded again. We revived him again.

I went to the patient waiting room and told his family what was going on. Their family member's heart kept stopping and we brought him back. I informed them that because of his condition he was going to die soon. They told me to continue to do everything. He coded repeatedly. I took one of the family members to the patient's bedside and said, "Mr. Smith [not actual name] is not going to survive; do you want us to continue to pound on his chest, breaking his ribs? Do you want us to continue to shock him?" The family member looked at his loved one and said, "No. If his heart stops again, let him go." Mr. Smith's heart did stop again; we let him go.

When the other family members in the waiting room heard that someone had told us to stop, there was almost a fistfight. "Why did you tell them to stop?! You killed him!" How would you like to live with that guilt? I went through the same ordeal when my father was comatose, after his stroke. His doctor told me that he was not going to survive. He asked did I want the full court press if his heart stopped? I said, "Yes, do everything." I did not want the guilt.

The secondary benefit of advanced directives is the tremendous cost savings in healthcare. Each year we spend billions of dollars on the resuscitation and temporary maintenance of individuals who virtually have zero chance of any meaningful recovery. Their loved ones want everything done to keep them alive, and the hospital and the doctors are bound by law to do everything, at a significant cost. Advance directives carry out the wishes of the victim, relieve the guilt of family members, and decrease the burden on the healthcare system by using mandated-advanced directives.

## PARTNERSHIP

Next let's turn our attention toward the doctor-patient relationship. There should be a mechanism put in place so that every single American spends twenty minutes with their primary-care provider semi-annually just in dialogue about proper healthcare maintenance. This visit has nothing to do with running tests or procedures or dealing with systematic problems. This visit is only about dialogue between the physicians and their patients regarding prevention, screening, nutrition, exercise, and healthy living. The physician should be compensated fairly for this encounter to reduce the stress of turning this twenty-minute planned encounter into a ten-minute session.

There are two constant complaints regarding the physician-patient relationship. Patients complain that they do not get a chance to speak with their doctor; they feel rushed during their visit. Doctors complain that they are not compensated fairly for the additional time they need to spend speaking with patients. These semi-annual twenty-minute doctor-patient encounters solve both problems. Dialogue between patient and physician has proved itself valuable today. The most effective tool to enable an individual to quit smoking is not the patch, the gum, or other prescription medications; its encouragement from one's physician. That is the power of physician-and-patient partnership via dialogue.

Scheduled patient-physician dialogue should also have a dramatic effect in two other areas; disease prevention and a decreased number of lawsuits. Yes, decreased litigation. Why is this? Prevention means decreased risk of increased morbidity and mortality, which obviously would directly translate into decreased litigation.

Secondarily, patients routinely do not sue doctors they like. Spending twenty quality minutes with your primary-care physician in dialogue about your health builds a bridge. It begins to build a relationship. It builds a partnership. Your doctor may actually know your name the next time you come to the office without first looking in the chart or referring to you as "the guy" in exam room four.

I see the value of relationships with my patients. I see the surprise on their faces when I remember something personal they may have told me on a prior visit about another family member or a situation at work. They smile and say, "Thank you very much for asking." They feel at ease. They feel their physician cares. There is no substitute for communication and a relationship between a patient and their physician. This takes time, but all good relationships take time. There is no quick fix here.

The plan outlined in this chapter addresses critical areas in our healthcare system I believe need to be explored and debated by people in positions to implement them: government, industry, and healthcare advocacy groups. This plan is a win-win situation for all involved. The plan calls for politicians to take a stand to fix healthcare or lose their jobs. The plan calls for reasonable monetary investment from those who would benefit most from bringing 47 million Americans into the healthcare system, i.e. hospitals, insurance companies, physicians, pharmaceutical companies, and other healthcare-delivery entities. Market forces drive this plan, not inefficient government bureaucracy.

This plan decreases healthcare spending since more access, prevention, and early medical intervention means less tertiary intervention in the form of expensive hospitalizations or ER visits. Advanced directives are mandated, which decreases family guilt and decreases spending on patients with no chance of survival, saving billions of dollars annually. Finally this plan builds partnerships between patients and physicians—partnerships that humanize the physician and personalize the patient.

# CHAPTER XIII
# THERE ARE A LOT OF DECISIONS TO BE MADE
## It's All up to You, McFly

If we really want to get a handle on the healthcare system, physicians need to step up to the plate. We see the patients, write the prescriptions, admit the patients, order the procedures, and perform operations. Physicians initiate the majority of the actions that turn the world of healthcare. You would think that since we control so many dollars we would be a little bit more involved in the economics of healthcare—or I should say the economics of healthcare policy. But, for reasons that I have outlined in earlier chapters, physicians just sit on the sidelines and let everyone else dictate care.

Physicians are going to have to accept the fact that reimbursements from insurance companies and the government for services rendered will not improve much in the future. Realistically, holding reimbursement rates at current levels should be considered a moral victory. We must diversify our revenue streams. Physicians trained in India now practicing in the U.S. seem to have a great grasp of this concept. I had the pleasure to spend some time with a group of U.S. doctors from India who had an interest in participating in a medical education program for foreign trained doctors. Dr. Mukkamala and Dr. Rao are very successful in their clinical practices. They also regularly participated in state and national medical associations and societies. As busy as they were, they found the time to invest together is several educational and entrepreneurial ventures outside medicine. That is the path for physicians today who wish to remain independent and continue in private practice. Physicians who continue to depend exclusively on insurance reimbursements to earn a living will inevitably have to close their practices and take a job with the government or mega-medical groups to remain personally financially solvent. "McFlys of the world-unite."

We need to get off the bench and in the game. Our patients need us to organize around a specific forward-thinking healthcare agenda and follow through on implementation. The key here is we have to speak as one body. We cannot break ranks and splinter off when it comes to decisions of determining what we want to prescribe to our patients, how long our patients are to remain in the hospital, what procedures our patients should get, or how much we should be reimbursed.

Strong representation to the general public, the insurance industry, the pharmaceutical industry, and to government regarding those fundamental issues is of paramount importance. In 2007 the pharmaceutical and insurance industries combined spent more than $200 million dollars to lobby in Washington.[33] The AMA lobby spent about $30 million for the same period. Yet the AMA represents a group that generates hundreds of billion of dollars in annual revenue.

You can speak to the average physician and they will tell you they know very little about what the American Medical Association is doing for them. That has to change. I have had some critical things to say about the American Medical Association and my perception that the organization lacked effectiveness in reaching and addressing the needs of physicians. I have not been a member of the AMA for a number of years now. Most of the physicians in my circle also were not members of the AMA. The number-one question most non-members asked was, what are they doing that's so important that I should pay five hundred dollars a year in membership dues, which doesn't include additional money to support their political action committee, PAC?

I decided to become an investigative reporter and see up close and personal what the AMA was doing for me, Joe Physician, at the nut-and-bolts level. I attended the AMA House of Delegate Conference in Hawaii November 2007. I am not a delegate representative for any organization. I went from section meeting to section meeting and sat in the back of the room, like a fly on the wall, and just listened. I must say I was pleasantly surprised.

The primary issue I care about most as a practicing family doc is access to healthcare for the underserved and the uninsured. I was happy see that the AMA, under the leadership of its president, Ronald Davis, MD, has developed a rather comprehensive campaign to reach all the candidates running for president and hold their feet to the fire in addressing healthcare. The AMA has also developed its own plan for getting healthcare to all Americans.

I had an opportunity to speak one on one with Dr. Davis. The first thing I can say about the man is that he was very approachable. To be honest that was surprising to me, considering this gentleman represents one of the most powerful groups in the country. We are at a tipping point in America when healthcare is one of the national big three issues, and his organization represents the individuals who stand in the doorway of all issues related to healthcare, physicians.

I was rather frank with Dr. Davis concerning my opinion that I did not believe the AMA represented me, Joe Physician, and my everyday survival needs in areas such as timely reimbursement from insurance companies, malpractice reform, and just assisting the everyday physician in opportunities that can increase revenue in our practices.

I know several physicians who struggle to keep their incomes from sliding year to year. They are also maxed out on their lines of credit and they cannot collect their money from insurance companies. Some may cry crocodile tears for a physician's financial plight, but when one has spent an average of twenty-four years in formal educational training, the last twelve years being very competitive and physically and mentally taxing, and one's life expectancy is shorter than the average American's, one earns every dollar one makes.

I asked Dr. Davis, "What is the AMA doing for the average physician?" I expected a canned political answer, a pat on the head, and then the handshake—you know, when a politician shakes your hand while he's not answering your question and moves you gradually move you away from him. Dr. Davis was quite the opposite. He was very sincere with his responses. He also encouraged me to attend various meeting and read the published AMA positions that addressed pertinent physician issues.

At one of the meetings I attended, I spoke with one of the AMA's board of trustee members, Rebecca Patchin, MD. I voiced my issues to her as well. Like Dr. Davis, she was very attentive to my concerns. She was a member of the recruiting committee and asked me what I think the AMA could do to reach the everyday physician.

Do not depend on mailed literature and blast emails to reach physicians, I told her. Get out there and press some flesh. Form AMA representative groups in every state that go from city to city personally meeting the people the AMA represents. It should be like hiring your own pharmaceutical representative force. This will cost money. I hate to use a cliché, but it takes money to make money. I find that a concept foreign to most doctors who refuse to spend a dime unless success is guaranteed. Success in business is never guaranteed, but any business, in order to survive, has to take calculated risks.

Doctors need help today getting our message to the government, healthcare industry, and the public. If you communicate your message affectively, doctors will buy; we have to. There are no other options. AMA, step outside the box. Find the money for the investment in your constituency. I would spend five to ten minutes speaking to an AMA rep before I spend the same time speaking to a drug rep. Tell us face to face what you are doing for us and ask for our support. Your investment should return to you twofold or better. Insanity is doing the same thing over and over again and expecting a different result.

The current AMA marketing strategy is not working. Less than 40 percent of doctors are members. Snail mail and e-mail campaigns are not cutting it. Ninety percent of most mail I get is viewed in less than thirty milliseconds. My common practice is to pile up the mound of glossy stuff I get every day from someone, or some group that wants to get my attention, and with a smooth tennis backhand motion, assist all of it into my circular file on the floor. I assume some of those materials are from the AMA.

Do not "market e-mail" me either. I spend less time looking at "market e-mails" than I spend reviewing mailed materials. There just isn't enough time. Between seeing patients in the office, seeing patients in the hospital, completing charts, refilling prescriptions, returning phone calls, reviewing labs, reviewing billing and collections, meeting with the staff, and speaking with drug reps all on a daily basis, there isn't enough time for much else. Eating and seeing our kids before bedtime are not daily guarantees.

Joe Physician has to see the passion I saw in everyone I spoke with at that AMA meeting—passion from the president to a delegate from Montana who spent four hours on the flight to Hawaii trying to convince me of the value of the AMA. That passion is worth five hundred dollars a year to me, and another five hundred a year in support of the AMA PAC.

With all that is going on in healthcare today, I do not believe the American Medical Association will have a greater opportunity to make its case to its constituents and grow its membership. That case cannot be made on paper; it needs to be made in person. I went to you to see for myself the value of the AMA; now I am a believer. Not everyone has the time and money to go to you though; you need to go to them and make them believers too. More believers mean more dues and PAC support. More PAC support means more money to lobby Congress. As with everything else, true AMA power to make a difference is all about economics, not enthusiasm.

Physicians have to take back the power of the pen. Far too often we are lured by the pharmaceutical industry to prescribe drugs that have no greater efficacy or better side-effect profiles than their generic counterparts. Drugs called statins have been used routinely for years in the treatment of high cholesterol. Hypercholesterolemia (high cholesterol) is a risk factor for heart attacks and strokes. The two main drugs in this country used to treat hypercholesterolemia are Lipitor and Zocor. We spend approximately $16 billion dollars per year on "statin" medications. Zocor is now available as a generic. Lipitor has better data than Zocor in a selected group of patients. Physicians have the clear choice of prescribing Lipitor, or Zocor at half the price.

The billion-dollar question here is, except for a selective group of patients, why the heck would we continue to prescribe Lipitor for routine hypercholesterolemia and not save about $8 billion a year by prescribing Zocor? Still, we are going to do it. We are going to do it because we have always done it. I guarantee you that the Lipitor folks are not going to sit back and just watch their market evaporate. In 2004 they spent more than $100 million on Lipitor advertisement. To protect their market share, they would spend even more. As a side note, makers of Lipitor and Crestor, another statin, combined to spend more than $300 million on advertising in 2004.[34] I don't think the industry will have much difficulty raising the $300 million I proposed spending on preventative public service ads.

Prescription drug costs have gone from $40 billion in 1990 to almost $250 billion today. Drug companies push their products to the public, who then push the physician, who crumbles and writes the prescriptions. That chain of events needs to change, and physicians have the mechanisms to control it. Those mechanisms are called a pen and a prescription pad. It also means spending one extra minute with your patient discussing the efficacy, the tolerability, and the affordability of generic substitutes.

We can demonstrate our power by not prescribing any drugs that are advertised on television unless doing so would harm our patient. This showing of solidarity would get everyone's attention, from the pharmaceutical industry to the government to Wall Street. The only question is whether we have the guts to pull it off. The goal here is not to bankrupt the U.S. pharmaceutical industry; it's to get their attention regarding excessive television advertisements. I am all for U.S. drug companies making all the money they can, but make it overseas, not here.

I have attempted to educate the average American about all the players in U.S. healthcare. I have also tried to illustrate several answers to solve several problems in the areas of access to healthcare insurance for the uninsured, medical education, a pending physician shortage, and the skyrocketing cost of healthcare. Those that must play the central role in turning our system around are the currently sidelined physicians. Most problems will require political and corporate involvement, but the physician has to be invited to the table or pay, like everyone else, to be there.

Will the uninsured, in order to make their medical needs a priority, let their political voices be heard and vote into office a president or a Congress that will hear them and respond? I do not know. Will our hero, the reluctant physician, George McFly, finally stand up to the Biffs of the pharmaceutical, insurance, hospital, and legal industries? (That's a lot of Biffs to battle.) I do not know. Will we wait fifteen years, until the physician shortage is a dangerous reality, before we act?

I hope, for the sake of all Americans, that years from now, books like this are well worn from use, as opposed to waiting until the crisis is upon us before they are desperately pulled off the bookshelf, dusted off, and read, someone saying, "Huh, we should have thought about some of these things fifteen years ago." Unfortunately I believe we will do nothing. Why? America is a country that can afford tragedy. We will merely continue to throw ungodly amounts of money at our healthcare problems because, like all our other economic problems, it is just what we do.

One of the most eye-opening examples of over-the-top U.S. spending is seen in the military budget. The 2008 military budget for the U.S. is more than $600 billion.[35] Based on 2004 date, the next two largest budgets belong to China and Russia at $65 billion and $50 billion respectively. The military spending for entire world combined is estimated at $500 billion. When it comes to the military, we outspend the world. The former Soviet Union's paranoia about being invaded or wiped off the face of the globe by the U.S. had them spending themselves into oblivion. They eventually imploded.

America is a country that can afford to spend ungodly amounts of money on healthcare, but for how much longer? Will the excessive healthcare spending of the United States be the equivalent of the excessive military spending of the former Soviet Union—spending that destroyed that country? Is healthcare spending our Achilles' heel? Is the biggest threat to this country terrorism or healthcare spending? Only time will tell.

# 110th Congress
# House of Representatives

**Alabama**
**Robert Aderholt** 4th
205 Fourth Ave
Ste 104
Cullman, AL 35055
**T:**2567346043
**F:**2567370885

**Spencer Bachus** 6th
1900 International Park Dr
Ste 107
Birmingham, AL 35243
**T:**2059692296
**F:**2059693958

**Jo Bonner** 1st
1302 North McKenzie
Foley, AL
**T:**2519432073
**F:**2519432093

**Arthur Davis** 7th
2 20th St North
Ste 1130
Birmingham, AL 35203
**T:**2052541960
**F:**2052541974

**Robert Cramer** 5th
200 Pratt Ave NE
Ste A
Huntsville, AL 35801
**T:**2565510190
**F:**2565510194

**Terry Everett** 2nd
3500 Eastern Blvd
Ste 250
Montgomery, AL 36616
**T:**3342779113
**F:**3342778534

**Mike Rogers** 3rd
1129 Noble St
104 Federal Bldg
Anniston, AL 36201
T:2562365655
F:2562379203

**Don Young**
510 L. St
Ste 580
Anchorage, AK 99501
T:9072715978
F:9072715950

**Arizona**
**Trent Franks** 2nd
7121 West Bell Rd
Ste 200
Glendale, AZ 85308
T:6237767911
F:6237767832

**Gabrielle Giffords** 8th
1661 N. Swan
Ste 112
Tuscon, AZ 85712
T:5208813588
F:5203229490

**Raul Grijalva** 7th
810 E. 22nd St
Ste 102
Tuscon, AZ 85713
T:5206226788
F:5206220198

**Jeff Flake** 6th
1640 South Stapley
Ste 215
Mesa, AZ 85204
T:4808330092
F:4808336314

**Harry Mitchell** 5th
7201 East Camelback Rd
Ste 335
Scottsdale, AZ 85251
T:4809462411
F:4809462446

**Ed Pastor** 4th
411 North Central Ave
Ste 150
Phoenix, AZ 85004
T:6022560551
F:6022579103

| | |
|---|---|
| **Rick Renzi** 1st<br>115 E. Deuce of Clubs<br>Ste A<br>Show Low, AZ 85901<br>**T:**9285372800<br>**F:**9285325008 | **John Shadegg** 3rd<br>301 E. Bethany Home Rd<br>Ste C-178<br>Phoenix, AZ 85012<br>**T:**6022635300<br>**F:**6022487733 |
| **Arkansas**<br>**Marion Berry** 1st<br>108 E. Huntington<br>Jonesboro, AR 72401<br>**T:**8709724600<br>**F:**8709724605 | **John Boozman** 3rd<br>213 W. Monroe<br>Ste K<br>Lowell, AR 72745<br>**T:**4797250400<br>**F:**4797250408 |
| **Mike Ross** 4th<br>300 Exchange ST<br>Ste A<br>Hot Springs National Park, AR 71901<br>**T:**5015205892<br>**F:**5015205873 | **Vic Sanders** 2nd<br>1501 North University<br>Ste 150<br>Little Rock, AR 72207<br>**T:**5013245941<br>**F:**5013246029 |
| **California**<br>**Joe Baca** 43rd<br>201 North E. St<br>Ste 102<br>San Bernardino, CA 92401<br>**T:**9098852222<br>**F:**9098885959 | **Xavier Becerra** 31st<br>1910 Sunset Blvd<br>Ste 810<br>Los Angeles, CA 90026<br>**T:**2134831425<br>**F:**2134831429 |

| | |
|---|---|
| **Howard Berman** 28th<br>14546 Hamlin St<br>Ste 202<br>Van Nuys, CA 91411<br>**T:**8189947200<br>**F:**8189941050 | **Brian Bilbray** 50th<br>462 Stevens Ave<br>Ste 107<br>Solana Beach, CA 92075<br>**T:**8583501150<br>**F:**8583500750 |
| **Mary Bono**<br>707 E. Tahquitz<br>Palm Springs, CA 92262<br>**T:**7603201076<br>**F:**7603200596 | **Ken Calvert** 44th<br>3400 Central Ave<br>Ste 200<br>Riverside, CA 92506<br>**T:**9517844300<br>**F:**9517845255 |
| **John Campbell** 48th<br>610 Newport Center Dr<br>Ste 330<br>Newport Beach, CA 92660<br>**T:**9497562244<br>**F:**9492519309 | **Lois Capps** 23rd<br>101 W Anapamu St<br>Ste C<br>Santa Barbara, CA 93101<br>**T:**8057301710<br>**F:**8057309153 |
| **Dennis Cardoza** 18th<br>2222 M St<br>Ste 305<br>Merced, CA 95340<br>**T:**2093834455<br>**F:**2097761065 | **Jim Costa** 20th<br>855 M St<br>Ste 940<br>Fresno, CA 93721<br>**T:**5594951620<br>**F:**5594951027 |
| **Susan Davis** 53rd<br>4305 University Ave<br>Ste 515<br>San Diego, CA 92105<br>**T:**6192805353<br>**F:**6192805311 | **John Doolittle** 4th<br>4230 Douglas Blvd<br>Ste 200<br>Granite Bay, CA 95746<br>**T:**9167865560<br>**F:**9167866364 |

| | |
|---|---|
| **David Dreier** 26th<br>510 East Foothill Blvd<br>Ste 201<br>San Dimas, CA 91773<br>**T:**9095756226<br>**F:**9095756266 | **Anna Eshoo** 14th<br>555 Bryant Street<br>PMB 335<br>Palo Alto, CA 94301<br>**T:**6503283700<br>**F:**4154955733 |
| **Sam Farr** 17th<br>701 Ocean St<br>Rm 318<br>Santa Cruz, CA 95060<br>**T:**8314291976<br>**F:**8314291458 | **Bob Filner** 51st<br>1101 Airport Rd<br>Ste D<br>Imperial, CA 92251<br>**T:**7603558800<br>**F:**7603558802 |
| **Elton Gallegly** 24th<br>2829 Townsgate Rd<br>Ste 315<br>Thousand Oaks, CA 91361<br>**T:**8054972224<br>**F:**8054970039 | **Jane Harman** 36th<br>2321 E. Rosecrans Ave<br>Ste 3270<br>El Segundo, CA 90245<br>**T:**3106433636<br>**F:**3106436445 |
| **Wally Herger** 2nd<br>55 Independence Cir<br>Ste 104<br>Chico, CA 95973<br>**T:**5308938363<br>**F:**5308938619 | **Mike Honda** 15th<br>1999 South Bascom Ave<br>Ste 815<br>Campbell, CA 95008<br>**T:**4085588085<br>**F:**4085588086 |
| **Duncun Hunter** 52nd<br>1870 Cordell Ct<br>Ste 206<br>El Cajon, CA 92020<br>**T:**6194485201<br>**F:**6194492251 | **Darrell Issa** 49th<br>1800 Thibodo Rd<br>#310<br>Vista, CA 92081<br>**T:**7605595000<br>**F:**7605991178 |

| | |
|---|---|
| **Tom Lantos** 12th<br>400 S. El Camino Real<br>San Mateo, CA 94402<br>**T:**6503420300<br>**F:**6503758270 | **Barbara Lee** 9th<br>1301 Clay St<br>Ste 1000-N<br>Oakland, CA 94612<br>**T:**5107630370<br>**F:**5107636538 |
| **Jerry Lewis** 41st<br>1150 Brookside Ave<br>Ste J-5<br>Redlands, CA 92373<br>**T:**9098626030<br>**F:**9093359155 | **Zoe Lofgren** 16th<br>635 N. First ST<br>Ste B<br>San Jose, CA 95112<br>**T:**4082718700<br>**F:**4082718713 |
| **Dan Lungren** 3rd<br>2339 Gold Meadow Way<br>Ste 220<br>Gold River, CA 95670<br>**T:**9168599906<br>**F:**9168599976 | **Buck McKeon** 25th<br>1008 W. Ave M-14<br>Ste E1<br>Palmdale, CA 93551<br>**T:**6612749688<br>**F:**6612748744 |
| **Doris Matsui** 5th<br>501 I St<br>Ste 12-600<br>Sacramento, CA 95814<br>**T:**9164985600<br>**F:**9164986117 | **Kevin McCarthy** 22nd<br>4110 Empire Dr<br>Ste 150<br>Bakersfield, CA 93309<br>**T:**6613273611<br>**F:**6616370867 |
| **Jerry McNerney** 11th<br>2222 Grand Canal Blvd<br># 7<br>Stockton, CA 95207<br>**T:**2094768552<br>**F:**2094768567 | **Gary Miller** 42nd<br>1800 E. Lambert Rd<br>Ste 150<br>Brea, CA 92821<br>**T:**7142571142<br>**F:**7142579242 |

| | |
|---|---|
| **George Miller** 7th<br>375 G St<br>Ste 1<br>Vallejo, CA 94592<br>**T:**7076451888<br>**F:**7076451870 | **Grace Napolitano** 38th<br>11627 East Telegraph Rd<br>Ste 100<br>Santa Fe Springs, CA 90670<br>**T:**5628012134<br>**F:**5629499144 |
| **Devin Nunes** 21st<br>264 Clovis Ave<br>Ste 206<br>Clovis, CA 93612<br>**T:**5593235235<br>**F:**5593235528 | **Nancy Pelosi** 8th<br>450 Golden Gate Ave<br>14th Flr<br>San Francisco, CA 94102<br>**T:**4155564862<br>**F:**4158611670 |
| **George Randanovich** 46th<br>1040 E. Herdon St<br>Ste 201<br>Fresno, CA 93720<br>**T:**5594492490<br>**F:**5594492499 | **Laura Richardson** 37th<br>970 West 190th St<br>E. Tower Ste 900<br>Torrence, CA 90502<br>**T:**3105381190<br>**F:**3105389672 |
| **Dana Rohrabacher** 46th<br>101 Main St<br>Ste 380<br>Huntington Beach, CA 92648<br>**T:**7149606483<br>**F:**7149607806 | **Lucille Roybal-Allard** 34th<br>255 E. Temple St<br>Ste 1860<br>Los Angeles, CA 90012<br>**T:**2136289230<br>**F:**2136288578 |
| **Ed Royce** 40th<br>305 N. Harbor Blvd<br>Ste 300<br>Fullerton, CA 92835<br>**T:**7149922801<br>**F:**7149921668 | **Linda Sanchez** 39th<br>17906 Crusader Ave<br>Ste 100<br>Cerritos, CA 90703<br>**T:**5628605050<br>**F:**5629242914 |

**Loretta Sanchez** 47th
12397 Lewis St
Ste 101
Garden Grove, CA 92840
**T:**7146210102
**F:**7146210401

**Adam Schiff** 29th
87 N Raymond Ave
# 800
Pasadena, CA 91103
**T:**6263042727
**F:**6263040572

**Brad Sherman** 27th
5000 Van Nuys Blvd
Ste 420
Sherman Oaks, CA 91403
**T:**8185019200
**F:**8185011554

**Hilda Solis** 32nd
4716 Cesar Chavez Ave
Bldg A
East Los Angeles, CA 90022
**T:**3233079904
**F:**3233079906

**Pete Stark** 13th
39300 Civic Center Dr
Ste 220
Fremont, CA 94538
**T:**5104941388
**F:**5104945852

**Ellen Tauscher** 10th
2121 North California Blvd
Ste 555
Walnut Creek, CA 94596
**T:**9259328899
**F:**9259328159

**Mike Thomas** 1st
1040 Main St
Ste 101
Napa, CA 94559
**T:**7072269898
**F:**7072519800

**Maxine Waters** 35th
10124 South Broadway
Ste 1
Los Angeles, CA 90003
**T:**3237578900
**F:**3237579506

**Diane Watson** 33rd
4322 Wilshire Blvd
Ste 302
Los Angeles, CA 90010
**T:**3239651422
**F:**3239651113

**Henry Waxman** 30th
8436 West Third St
Ste 600
Los Angeles, CA 90048
**T:**3236511040
**F:**3236550502

**Lynn Woolsey** 6th
1050 Northgate Dr
Ste 354
San Rafeal, CA 94903
**T:**4155079554
**F:**4155079601

**Colorado**
**Diana Degette** 1st
600 Grant ST
Ste 202
Denver, CO 80203
**T:**3038444988
**F:**3038444996

**Doug Lamborn** 5th
3730 Sinton Rd
Ste 150
Colorado Springs, CO 80907
**T:**7195200055
**F:**7195200840

**Marilyn Musgrave** 4th
636 Coffman St
Ste 205
Longmont, CO 80501
**T:**7204944336
**F:**7204941768

**Ed Permutter** 7th
12600 West Colfax Ave
Ste B-400
Lakewood, CO 80215
**T:**3032747944
**F:**3032746455

**John Salazar** 3rd
134 West B St
Pueble, CO 81003
**T:**7195438200
**F:**7195438204

**Tom Tancredo** 6th
6099 S. Quebec St
Ste 200
Centennial, CO 80111
**T:**7202839772
**F:**7202839776

**Mark Udall** 6th
8601 Turnpike Dr
Ste 206
Westminister, CO 80031
**T:**3036507820
**F:**3036507827

**Connecticut**
**Joe Courtney** 2nd
101 Water St
Ste 301
Norwich, CT 06360
**T:**8608860139
**F:**8608862974

**Rosa DeLauro** 3rd
59 Elm St
New Haven, CT 06510
**T:**2035623718
**F:**2037722260

**John Larson** 1st
221 Main St
2nd Flr
Hartford, CT 06106
**T:**8602788888
**F:**8602782111

**Christopher Murphy** 5th
1 Grove St
New Britian, CT 06053
**T:**8602238412
**F:**8608279009

**Christopher Shays** 4th
10 Middle St
11th Flr
Bridgeport, CT 06604
**T:**2035795870
**F:**2035790771

District of Columbia
**Eleanor Holmes Norton**
2041 Martin Luther King Jr SE
Ste 238
Washington, DC 20020
**T:**2026788900
**F:**2026788844

Delaware
**Mike Castle**
201 N. Walnut St
Ste 107
Wilmington, DE 19801
**T:**3024281902
**F:**3024281950

Florida
**Gus Bilirakis** 9th
10941 N 56th St
Temple Terrace, FL 33617
**T:**8139858541
**F:**8139850714

**Allen Boyd** 2nd
30 W. Government St
Ste 203
Panama City, FL 32401
**T:**8507850812
**F:**8507633724

**Corrine Brown** 3rd
101 E. Union St
Ste 202
Jacksonville, FL 32202
**T:**9043541652
**F:**9043542721

**Virginia Ginny-Brown** 5th
15000 Citrus County Dr
Unit 100
Dade City, FL 33523
**T:**3525676707
**F:**3525676259

**Vern Buchanan** 13th
235 N. Orange Ave
Ste 201
Sarasota, FL 34205
**T:**9417479081
**F:**9417481564

| | |
|---|---|
| **Ander Crenshaw** 4th<br>1061 Riverside Ave<br>Ste 100<br>Jacksonville, FL 32204<br>**T:**9045980481<br>**F:**9045980486 | **Kathy Castor** 11th<br>4144 N Armenia Ave<br>Ste 300<br>Tampa, FL 33607<br>**T:**8138712817<br>**F:**8138712864 |
| **Lincoln Diaz-Balart** 21st<br>8525 Northwest 53rd<br>Terrace Ste 102<br>Miami, FL 33166<br>**T:**3054708555<br>**F:**3054708575 | **Mario Diaz-Balart** 25th<br>12851 SW 42nd St<br>Ste 131<br>Miami, FL 33175<br>**T:**3052256866<br>**F:**3052257432 |
| **Tom Freeney** 24th<br>12424 Research Pkwy<br>Ste 135<br>Orlando, FL 32826<br>**T:**4072081106<br>**F:**4072081108 | **Alcee Hastings**<br>2701 W. Oakland Park Blvd<br>Ste 200<br>Fort Lauderdale, FL 33311<br>**T:**9547332800<br>**F:**9547359444 |
| **Ric Keller** 8th<br>605 East Robinson St<br>Ste 650<br>Orlando, FL 32801<br>**T:**4078721962<br>**F:**4078721944 | **Ron Klein** 22nd<br>800 East Broward Blvd<br>Ste 300<br>Ft. Lauderdale, FL 33301<br>**T:**9545224579<br>**F:**9545224965 |
| **Connie Mack** 14th<br>805 Nicholas Pkwy E<br>Ste 1<br>Cape Coral, FL 33990<br>**T:**2395735837<br>**F:**2395739125 | **Tim Mahoney** 16th<br>9 SE Osceola St<br>Stuart, FL 34994<br>**T:**7728781381<br>**F:**7728710651 |

| | |
|---|---|
| **Kendrick Meek** 17th<br>111 NW 183rd St<br>Ste 315<br>Miami Gardens, FL 33169<br>**T:**3056905905<br>**F:**3056905951 | **John Mica** 7th<br>613 St. Johns Ave<br>Rm 107<br>Palatka, FL 32177<br>**T:**3863281622<br>**F:** |
| **Jeff Miller** 1st<br>4300 Bayou Blvd<br>Ste 13<br>Pensacola, FL 32503<br>**T:**8504791183<br>**F:**85004799394 | **Adam Putnam** 12th<br>650 East Davidson St<br>Bartow, FL 33830<br>**T:**8635343530<br>**F:**8635343559 |
| **Ileana Ros-Lehtinen** 18th<br>8660 West Flagler ST<br>Ste 131<br>Miami, FL 33144<br>**T:**3052203281<br>**F:**3052203291 | **Cliff Stearns** 6th<br>115 SE 25th Ave<br>Oscala, FL 34471<br>**T:**3523518777<br>**F:**3523518011 |
| **Dave Weldon** 15th<br>2725 Judge Fran Jamieson Way<br>Bldg C<br>Melbourne, FL 32940<br>**T:**3216321776<br>**F:**3216398595 | **Debbie Wasserman Schultz** 20th<br>10100 Pines Blvd<br>Pembroke Pines, FL 33026<br>**T:**9544373936<br>**F:**9544374776 |
| **CW Bill Young** 10th<br>9210 113th St<br>Seminole, FL 33772<br>**T:**7273946950<br>**F:**7273946955 | **Robert Wexler** 19th<br>2500 North Military Trail<br>Ste 490<br>Boca Raton, FL 33431<br>**T:**5619886302<br>**F:**5619886423 |

**Georgia**
**John Barrow** 12th
450 Mall Blvd
Ste A
Savannah, GA 31406
**T:**9123547282
**F:**9123547782

**Sanford Bishop Jr** 2nd
235 Roosevelt Ave
Ste 114
Albany, GA 31701
**T:**2294398067
**F:**2294362099

**Nathan Deal** 9th
415 E Walnut Ave
Dalton, GA 30721
**T:**7062265320
**F:**7062780840

**Phil Gingrey** 11th
219 Roswell St
Marietta, GA 30060
**T:**7704291776
**F:**7707959551

**Henry Johnson** 4th
5700 Hillandale Dr
Ste 110
Lithonia, GA 30058
**T:**7709872291
**F:**7709878721

**Jack Kingston** 1st
1 Diamond Causeway
Ste 7
Savannah, GA 31406
**T:**9123520101
**F:**9123520105

**John Lewis** 5th
100 Peachtree St NW
Ste 1920
Atlanta, GA 30303
**T:**4046590116
**F:**4043310947

**John Linder** 7th
**T:**7702323005
**F:**7702322909

**Jim Marshall** 8th
130 East 1st St
Tifton, GA 31794
**T:**2295567418
**F:**4784640277

**Tom Price** 6th
3730 Roswell Rd
Ste 50
Marietta, GA 30114
**T:**7705654990
**F:**7705657570

**Paul Broun** 10th
4246 Washington Rd
Ste 6
Evans, GA 30809
**T:**7065499588
**F:**7065499590

**Lynn Westmoreland** 3rd
1601 B East Hwy 34
Newnan, GA 30265
**T:**7706382033
**F:**7706832042

**David Scott** 13th
173 North Main St
Jonesboro, GA 30236
**T:**7702105073
**F:**7702105673

**Hawaii**
**Neil Abercrombie** 1st
300 Ala Moana Blvd
Rm 4-104
Honolulu, HI 96850
**T:**8085412570
**F:**8085530133

**Mazie Hirono** 2nd
5104 Prince Kuhio Bldg
300 Ala Moana Blvd
Honolulu, HI 96813
**T:**8085411986
**F:**8085380233

**Iowa**
**Leonard Boswell** 3rd
300 East Locust
Ste 320
Des Moines, IA 50309
**T:**5152821909
**F:**5152821785

**Bruce Braley** 1st
501 Sycamore St
Ste 623
Waterloo, IA 50703
**T:**3192873233
**F:**3192875104

**Steve King** 5th
40 Pearl St
Council Bluffs, IA 51503
**T:**7123251404
**F:**7123251405

**Dave Loebsack** 2nd
125 South Dubuque St
Iowa City, IA 52240
**T:**3193510789
**F:**3193515789

**Tom Lathan** 4th
1421 South Bell Ave
Ste 108A
Ames, IA 50010
**T:**5152322885
**F:**5152322844

**Idaho**
**Bill Sali** 1st
802 W Bannock
Ste 101
Boise, ID 83702
T:2083369831
F:2083369891

**Mike Simpson** 2nd
802 W Bannock
Ste 600
Boise, ID 83702
T:2083341953
F:2083349533

**Illinois**
**Melissa Bean** 8th
1622 E Algonquin Rd
Ste L
Schaumburg, IL 60173
T:8479250265
F:8479250288

**Judy Biggert** 13th
6262 South Route 83
Ste 305
Willowbrook, IL 60527
T:6306552052
F:6306551061

**Jerry Costello** 12th
144 Lincoln Place Ct
Ste 4
Belleville, IL 62221
T:6182338026
F:6182338765

**Danny Davis** 7th
3333 West Arlington St
Ste 130
Chicago, IL 60624
T:7735337520
F:7735337530

**Rahm Emanuel** 5th
3742 West Irving Park Rd
Chicago, IL 60618
T:7732675926
F:7732676583

**Luis Gutierrez** 4th
2201 W North Ave
Chicago, IL 60647
T:7733420774
F:7733420776

**Bill Foster** 14th
119 W First St
Dixon, IL 22407
T:5405481086
F:5405481658

**Phil Hare** 17th
236 North Water St
# 765
Decatur, IL 62523
T:2174229150
F:2174229245

| | |
|---|---|
| **Jesse Jackson Jr** 2nd<br>7121 S Yates Blvd<br>Chicago, IL 60649<br>**T:**7737349660<br>**F:**7737349661 | **Timothy Johnson** 15th<br>2004 Fox Dr<br>Champaign, IL 61820<br>**T:**2174034690<br>**F:**2174034691 |
| **Mark Kirk** 10th<br>707 Skokie Blvd<br>Ste 350<br>Northbrook, IL 60062<br>**T:**8479400202<br>**F:**8479407143 | **Ray LaHood** 18th<br>100 NE Monroe<br>Rm 100<br>Peoria, IL 61602<br>**T:**3096717027<br>**F:**3096717309 |
| **Daniel Lipinski** 3rd<br>6245 South Archer Ave<br>Chicago, IL 60638<br>**T:**3128860481<br>**F:**7737679395 | **Peter Roskam** 6th<br>150 S Bloomingdale Rd<br>Ste 200<br>Bloomingdale, IL 60108<br>**T:**6308939670<br>**F:**6308939735 |
| **Donald Manzullo** 16th<br>415 S Mulford Rd<br>Rockford, IL 61108<br>**T:**8153941231<br>**F:**8153943930 | **Jan Schakowsky** 9th<br>5533 N. Broadway<br>Chicago, IL 60640<br>**T:**7735067100<br>**F:**7735069202 |
| **Bobby Rush** 1st<br>700-706 E 79th St<br>Chicago, IL 60619<br>**T:**7732246500<br>**F:**7732249624 | **John Shimkus** 19th<br>240 Regency Centre<br>Collinsville, IL 62234<br>**T:**6183443065<br>**F:**6183444215 |

**Jerry Weller** 11th
2710 Black Rd
Ste 201
Joilet, IL 60435
**T:**8157402028
**F:**8157402037

**Steve Buyer** 4th
100 S Main St
Monticello, IN 47960
**T:**5745839819
**F:**

**Joe Donnelly** 2nd
207 West Colfax Ave
South Bend, IN 46601
**T:**5742882780
**F:**5742882825

**Baron Hill** 9th
279 Quartermaster Ct
Jefferson, IN 47130
**T:**8122883999
**F:**8122883873

**Mark Souder** 3rd
320 N Chicago Ave
Ste 9B
Goshen, IN 46528
**T:**5745335802
**F:**5745342669

**Indiana**
**Dan Burton** 5th
8900 Keystone at the Crossing
Ste 1050
Indianapolis, IN 46952
**T:**7656626770
**F:**7656626775

**Andre' Carson** 7th
300 E Fall Creek Pkwy N
#300
Indianapolis, IN 46205
**T:**3172836516
**F:**3172836567

**Brad Ellsworth** 8th
901 Wabash Ave
Ste 140
Terre Haute, IN 47807
**T:**8122320523
**F:**8122320526

**Mike Pence** 6th
50 North 5th St
Richmond, IN 47374
**T:**7659622883
**F:**7659623225

**Peter Visclosky** 1st
701 E 83rd Ave
Ste 9B
Merrillville, IN 46410
**T:**2197951844
**F:**2197951850

**Kansas**
**Nancy Boyda** 2nd
510 SW 10th Ave
Topeka, KS 66612
**T:**7852348111
**F:**7852349111

**Dennis Moore** 3rd
500 State Ave
#176
Kansas City, KS 66101
**T:**9136210832
**F:**9136211533

**Jerry Moran** 1st
1200 Main St
Ste 402
Hays, KS 67601
**T:**7856286401
**F:**7856283791

**Todd Tiahrt** 4th
155 N Market St
Ste 400
Wichita, KS 67202
**T:**3162628992
**F:**3162625309

**Kentucky**
**Ben Chandler** 6th
1010 Monarch St
Ste 310
Lexington, KY 40513
**T:**8592191366
**F:**8592193437

**Geoff Davis** 4th
1405 Greenup Ave
Ste 236
Ashland, KY 41101
**T:**6063249898
**F:**6063259866

**Ron Lewis** 2nd
1001 Center St
Ste 300
Bowling Green, KY 42101
**T:**2708429896
**F:**2707661580

**Harold Rogers** 5th
601 Main St
Hazard, KY 41701
**T:**6064390794
**F:**6064394647

**Ed Whitfield** 1st
1403 S Main St
Hopkinsville, KY 42240
**T:**2708858079
**F:**2708855898

**John Yarmuth** 3rd
7219 Dixie Hwy
Louisville, KY 40258
**T:**5029335863
**F:**5029356934

**Louisiana**
**Rodney Alexander** 5th
1900 Stubbs Ave
Ste B
Monroe, LA 71201
**T:**3183223500
**F:**3183223577

**Vacant** 6th
5555 Hilton Ave
Ste 100
Baton Rouge, LA 70808
**T:**2259297711
**F:**2259297688

**Charles Boustany** 7th
700 Ryan St
Lake Charles, LA 70510
**T:**3372356322
**F:**3372356072

**William Jefferson** 2nd
500 Poydras St
New Orleans, LA 70130
**T:**5045892274
**F:**5045894513

**Vacant** 1st
3525 Causeway Blvd
Ste 1020
Metairie, LA 70002
**T:**5048371259
**F:**

**Charlie Melancon** 3rd
423 Lafayette St
Ste 107
Houma, LA 70360
**T:**9858763033
**F:**9858724449

**Jim McCrery** 4th
1606 S Fifth St
Leesville, LA 71446
**T:**3372380778
**F:**3372380566

**Massachusetts**
**Michael Capuano** 8th
110 First St
Cambridge, MA 2141
**T:**6176216208
**F:**6176218628

**William Delahunt** 10th
146 Main St
Hyannis, MA 2601
**T:**5087710666
**F:**5087901959

**Barney Frank** 4th
29 Crafts St
Newton, MA 2458
**T:**6173323920
**F:**6173322822

**Stephen Lynch** 9th
88 Black Falcon Ave
Ste 340
Boston, MA 2210
**T:**6174282000
**F:**6174282011

**James McGovern** 3rd
34 Mechanic St
Worcester, MA 1608
**T:**5088317356
**F:**5087540982

**Ed Markey** 7th
5 High St
Ste 101
Medford, MA 2155
**T:**7813962900
**F:**7813963220

**Richard Neal** 2nd
4 Congress St
Milford, MA 1757
**T:**5086348198
**F:**5086348398

**John Oliver** 1st
78 Center St
Pittsfield, MA 1202
**T:**4134420946
**F:**4134432792

**John Tierney** 6th
17 Peabody Sq
Peabody, MA 1960
**T:**9785311669
**F:**9785311996

**Niki Tsongas** 5th
305 Essex St
4th Flr
Lawrence, MA 1840
**T:**9786816200
**F:**9786826070

**Maryland**
**Roscoe Bartlett** 6th
1 Frederick St
Ste 2
Cumberland, MD 21502
**T:**3017243105
**F:**3017243538

**Elijah Cummings** 7th
101 Park Ave
Ste 105
Baltimore, MD 21201
**T:**4106859199
**F:**4106859399

**Wayne Gilchrest** 1st
315 High St
#105
Chestertown, MD 21620
**T:**4107789407
**F:**4107584059

| | |
|---|---|
| **Steny Hoyer** 5th<br>6500 Cherrywood Ln<br>Ste 310<br>Greenbelt, MD 20770<br>**T:**3014740119<br>**F:**3014744697 | **Dutch Ruppersberger** 2nd<br>375 West Padonia Rd<br>Ste 200<br>Timonium, MD 21093<br>**T:**4106282701<br>**F:**4106282708 |
| **John Sarbanes** 3rd<br>600 Baltimore Ave<br>Ste 303<br>Towson, MD 21204<br>**T:**4108328890<br>**F:**4108328898 | **Chris VanHollen** 8th<br>51 Monroe St<br>Ste 507<br>Rockville, MD 20850<br>**T:**3014243501<br>**F:**3014245995 |
| **Albert Wynn** 4th<br>9200 Basil Ct<br>Ste 221<br>Largo, MD 20774<br>**T:**3017734094<br>**F:**3019259694 | **Maine**<br>**Tom Allen** 1st<br>57 Exchange St<br>Ste 302<br>Portland, ME 04101<br>**T:**2077745019<br>**F:**2078710720 |
| **Michael Michaud** 2nd<br>23 Water St<br>Ste 205<br>Bangor, ME 04401<br>**T:**2079426935<br>**F:**2079425907 | **Michigan**<br>**Dave Camp** 4th<br>135 Ashman Dr<br>Midland, MI 48640<br>**T:**9896312552<br>**F:**9896316271 |
| **John Conyers Jr** 14th<br>2615 W Jefferson<br>Trenton, MI 48183<br>**T:**7346754084<br>**F:**7346754218 | **John Dingell** 15th<br>23 East Front St<br>Ste 103<br>Monroe, MI 48161<br>**T:**7342431849<br>**F:** |

| | |
|---|---|
| **Vern Ehlers** 3rd<br>110 Michigan St<br>Grand Rapids, MI 49503<br>**T:**6164518383<br>**F:**6164545630 | **Pete Hoekstra** 2nd<br>184 South River Ave<br>Holland, MI 49423<br>**T:**6163950030<br>**F:**6163950271 |
| **Dale Kildee** 5th<br>432 N Saginaw St<br>Ste 410<br>Flint, MI 48502<br>**T:**8102391437<br>**F:**8102391439 | **Carolyn Cheeks Kilpatrick**<br>13th<br>1274 Library<br>Ste 1-B<br>Detroit, MI 48226<br>**T:**3139659004<br>**F:**3139659006 |
| **Joseph Knollenberg** 9th<br>30833 Northwestern Hwy<br>Ste 100<br>Farmington Hills, MI 48334<br>**T:**2488511366<br>**F:**2488510418 | **Sandy Levin** 12th<br>27085 Gratiot Ave<br>Roseville, MI 48066<br>**T:**5864987122<br>**F:**5864987123 |
| **Thaddeus McCotter** 11th<br>213 W Huron St<br>Milford, MI 48381<br>**T:**2486859495<br>**F:**2486859484 | **Candice Miller** 10th<br>48653 Van Dyke Ave<br>Shelby Township, MI 48317<br>**T:**5869975010<br>**F:**5866995013 |
| **Mike Rogers** 8th<br>1327 E Michigan Ave<br>Lansing, MI 48912<br>**T:**5177028000<br>**F:**5177028642 | **Bart Stupak** 1st<br>111 E Chisholm<br>Alpena, MI 49707<br>**T:**9893560690<br>**F:**9893560923 |

| | |
|---|---|
| **Fred Upton** 6th<br>157 South Kalamazoo Mall<br>Ste 180<br>Kalamazoo, MI 49007<br>**T:**2693850039<br>**F:**2693852888 | **Timothy Walberg** 7th<br>800 West Ganson<br>Jackson, MI 49202<br>**T:**5177809075<br>**F:**5177809081 |
| **Minnesota**<br>**Michelle Bachman** 6th<br>6043 Hudson Rd<br>Ste 330<br>Woodbury, MN 55125<br>**T:**6517315400<br>**F:**6517316650 | **Keith Ellison** 5th<br>2100 Pymouth Ave N<br>Minneapolis, MN 55411<br>**T:**6125221212<br>**F:**6125229915 |
| **John Klein** 2nd<br>101 W Burnsville Pkwy<br>Burnsville, MN 55337<br>**T:**9528081213<br>**F:**9528081261 | **Betty McCollum** 4th<br>165 Western Ave N<br>Ste 14<br>St Paul, MN 55102<br>**T:**6512249191<br>**F:**6512243056 |
| **James Oberstar** 8th<br>38625 14th Ave<br>Ste 300B<br>North Branch, MN 55056<br>**T:**6512771234<br>**F:**6512771235 | **Collin Peterson** 7th<br>714 Lake Ave<br>Ste 107<br>Detroit Lake, MN 56501<br>**T:**2188475056<br>**F:**2188475109 |
| **Jim Ramstad** 3rd<br>1809 Plymouth Rd S<br># 300<br>Minnetonka, MN 55305<br>**T:**9527388200<br>**F:**9527389362 | **Timothy Walz** 1st<br>227 E Main St<br># 220<br>Mankato, MN 56001<br>**T:**5073882149<br>**F:**5073886181 |

**Missouri**

**Todd Akin** 2nd
301 Sovereign Ct
Ste 201
St Louis, MO 63011
**T:**3145900029
**F:**3145900037

**Roy Blunt** 7th
2740-B E Sunshine
Springfield, MO 65804
**T:**4178891800
**F:**4178894915

**Russ Carnahan** 3rd
8764 Manchester Rd
Ste 203
St Louis, MO 63144
**T:**3149621523
**F:**3149627169

**Wm. Lacy Clay** 1st
625 North Euclid St
#326
St Louis, MO 63108
**T:**3143671970
**F:**3143671341

**Emanuel Cleaver II** 5th
101 W 31st St
Kansas City, MO 64108
**T:**8168424545
**F:**8164715215

**JoAnn Emerson** 8th
339 Broadway
Cape Girardeau, MO 63701
**T:**5733350101
**F:**5733351931

**Sam Graves** 6th
201 S 8th St
Rm 330
St Joseph, MO 64501
**T:**8162339818
**F:**8162339848

**Kenny Hulshof** 9th
201 N 3rd St
Ste 240
Columbia, MO 65203
**T:**5734495111
**F:**5734495312

**Ike Skelton** 4th
219 N Adams St
Lebanon, MO 65536
**T:**4175327964
**F:**

**Mississippi**

**Chip Pickering** 3rd
110 D Airport Rd
Pearl, MS 39208
**T:**6019322410
**F:**6019654598

| | |
|---|---|
| **Gene Taylor** 4th<br>2 Depot Way<br>Bay St Louis, MS 39520<br>T:2284699235<br>F:2284699291 | **Bennie Thompson** 2nd<br>3607 Medgar Evers Blvd<br>Jackson, MS 39213<br>T:6019469003<br>F:60198256337 |
| **Vacant** 1st<br>523 Main St<br>Columbus, MS 39701<br>T:6623270748<br>F: | **Montana**<br>**Dennis Rehberg**<br>1201 Grand Ave<br>Ste 1<br>Billings, MT 59102<br>T:4062561019<br>F:4062564934 |
| **Nebraska**<br>**Jeff Fortenberry** 1st<br>125 S 4th St<br>Ste 101<br>Norfolk, NE 68508<br>T:4024381598<br>F:4024381604 | **Adrian Smith** 3rd<br>416 Valley View Dr<br>Ste 600<br>Scottsbluff, NE 69361<br>T:3086336333<br>F:3086336335 |
| **Lee Terry** 2nd<br>11717 Burt St<br>Ste 106<br>Omaha, NE 68154<br>T:4023979944<br>F:4023978787 | **Nevada**<br>**Shelly Berkley** 1st<br>2340 Paseo Del Prado<br>Ste D-106<br>Las Vegas, NV 89102<br>T:7022209823<br>F:7022209841 |
| **Dean Heller** 2nd<br>400 S Virginia St<br>Ste 502<br>Reno, NV 89501<br>T:7756865760<br>F:7756865711 | **Jon Porter** 3rd<br>2470 St Rose Pkwy<br>Ste 204<br>Henderson, NV 89074<br>T:7023874941<br>F:7024341378 |

| | |
|---|---|
| **Paul Hodes** 2nd<br>147 Main St<br>Nashua, NH 03060<br>**T:**6035796913<br>**F:**6035796916 | **Carol Shea Porter** 1st<br>104 Washington St<br>Dover, NH 03820<br>**T:**6037434813<br>**F:**6037435956 |
| **New Jersey**<br>**Robert Andrews** 1st<br>506 A White Horse Pike<br>Haddon Heights, NJ 08035<br>**T:**8565465100<br>**F:**8565469529 | **Michael Ferguson** 7th<br>45 Mountain Blvd<br>Bldg D<br>Warren, NJ 07059<br>**T:**9087577835<br>**F:**9087577841 |
| **Rodney Frelinghuysen** 11th<br>30 Schuyler Place<br>2nd Flr<br>Morristown, NJ 07960<br>**T:**9739840711<br>**F:**9732921569 | **Scott Garrett** 5th<br>93 Main St<br>Newton, NJ 07860<br>**T:**9733002000<br>**F:**9733001051 |
| **Rush Holt** 12th<br>50 Washington Rd<br>West Windsor, NJ 08550<br>**T:**6097509364<br>**F:**6097500618 | **Frank LoBiondo** 2nd<br>5914 Main St<br>Mags Landing, NJ 08330<br>**T:**6096255008<br>**F:**6096255071 |
| **Frank Pallone** 6th<br>504 Broadway<br>Long Branch, NJ 08753<br>**T:**7325711140<br>**F:**7328703890 | **Bill Pascreu** 8th<br>200 Federal Plaza<br>Ste 500<br>Paterson, NJ 07505<br>**T:**9735235152<br>**F:**9735230637 |

| | |
|---|---|
| **Donald Payne** 10th<br>50 Walnut St<br>Rm 1016<br>Newark, NJ 07102<br>**T:**9736453213<br>**F:**9736455902 | **Steven Rothman** 9th<br>130 Central Ave<br>Jersey City, NJ 07306<br>**T:**2017981366<br>**F:**2017981725 |
| **Jim Saxton** 3rd<br>247 Main St<br>Toms River, NJ 08753<br>**T:**7329142020<br>**F:**7329148351 | **Albio Sires** 13th<br>35 Journal Square<br>Ste 906<br>Jersey City, NJ 07306<br>**T:**2012222828<br>**F:**2012220188 |
| **Chris Smith** 4th<br>108 Lacy Rd<br>Ste 38A<br>Whiting, NJ 08759<br>**T:**7323502300<br>**F:**7323506260 | **New Mexico**<br>**Steve Pearce** 2nd<br>1717 West 2nd St<br>Ste 100<br>Roswell, NM 88201<br>**T:**5056220055<br>**F:**5056259608 |
| **Tom Udall** 3rd<br>811 St Michael's Dr<br>Ste 104<br>Santa Fe, NM 87505<br>**T:**5059848950<br>**F:**5059865047 | **Heather Wilson** 1st<br>20 First Plaza<br>Ste 603<br>Albuquerque, NM 87102<br>**T:**5053466781<br>**F:**50543466723 |
| **New York**<br>**Gary Ackerman** 5th<br>218-14 Northern Blvd<br>Bayside, NY 11361<br>**T:**7184232154<br>**F:**7184235053 | **Michael Arcuri** 24th<br>17 E Genesee St<br>Auburn, NY 13021<br>**T:**3152522777<br>**F:**3152522779 |

| | |
|---|---|
| **Timothy Bishop** 1st<br>137 Hampton Rd<br>Southampton, NY 11968<br>**T:**6312598450<br>**F:**6312598451 | **Yvette Clark** 11th<br>123 Linden Blvd<br>4th Flr Ste 200<br>Brooklyn, NY 11226<br>**T:**7182871142<br>**F:**7182871223 |
| **Joseph Crowley** 7th<br>177 Dreiser Loop<br>Bronx, NY 10475<br>**T:**7183202314<br>**F:**7183205095 | **Eliot Engel** 17th<br>3655 Johnson Ave<br>Bronx, NY 10463<br>**T:**7187969700<br>**F:**7187965134 |
| **Vito Fossella** 13th<br>8505 4th Ave<br>Brooklyn, NY 11209<br>**T:**7186305277<br>**F:**7186305388 | **Kristen Gillibrand** 20th<br>446 Warren St<br>Hudson, NY 12534<br>**T:**5188283109<br>**F:**5188283985 |
| **John Hall** 19th<br>255 Main St<br>Rm 3232G<br>Goshen, NY 10924<br>**T:**8452914100<br>**F:**8452914164 | **Brian Higgins** 27th<br>726 Exchange St<br>Ste 601<br>Buffalo, NY 14210<br>**T:**7168523501<br>**F:**7168523929 |
| **Maurice Hinchey** 22nd<br>100A Federal Bldg<br>Binghampton, NY 13901<br>**T:**6077732768<br>**F:** | **Steve Israel** 2nd<br>150 Motor Pkwy<br>Ste 108<br>Hauppauge, NY 11788<br>**T:**6319512210<br>**F:**6319513308 |

| | |
|---|---|
| **Pete King** 3rd<br>1003 Park Blvd<br>Massapequa Park, NY 11762<br>**T:**5165414225<br>**F:**5165416602 | **Randy Kuhl** 29th<br>220 Packett's Landing<br>Fairport, NY 14450<br>**T:**5852234760<br>**F:**5852232328 |
| **Nita Lowey** 18th<br>222 Mamaroneck Ave<br># 310<br>White Plains, NY 10605<br>**T:**9144281707<br>**F:**9143281505 | **Carolyn McCarthy** 4th<br>200 Garden City Plaza<br>Ste 320<br>Garden City, NY 11530<br>**T:**5167393008<br>**F:**5167392973 |
| **John McHugh** 23rd<br>120 Washington St<br>Watertown, NY 13601<br>**T:**3157823150<br>**F:**3157821291 | **Michael MuNulty** 21st<br>376 Broadway<br>Ste 2<br>Schenectady, NY 12305<br>**T:**5183744547<br>**F:**5183747908 |
| **Carolyn Maloney** 14th<br>1651 3rd Ave<br>Ste 311<br>New York, NY 10128<br>**T:**2128600606<br>**F:**2128600704 | **Gregory Meeks** 6th<br>1931 Mott Ave<br>Rm 305<br>Far Rockaway, NY 11691<br>**T:**7183279791<br>**F:**7183274722 |
| **Jerrold Nadler** 8th<br>445 Neptune Ave<br>Brooklyn, NY 11224<br>**T:**7183733198<br>**F:**7189960039 | **Charles Rangel** 15th<br>163 West 125th St<br>Ste 737<br>New York, NY 10027<br>**T:**2126633900<br>**F:**2126634277 |

| | |
|---|---|
| **Thomas Reynolds** 26th<br>1577 West Ridge Rd<br>Greece, NY 14615<br>**T:**5856635570<br>**F:**5856635711 | **Louise Slaughter** 28th<br>465 Main St<br>Ste 105<br>Buffalo, NY 14203<br>**T:**7168535813<br>**F:**7168536347 |
| **Jose Serrano** 16th<br>788 Southern Blvd<br>Bronx, NY 10455<br>**T:**7186200084<br>**F:**7186200658 | **Nydia Velazquez** 12th<br>173 Avenue B<br>New York, NY 10009<br>**T:**2126733997<br>**F:**2124735242 |
| **Edolphus Towns** 10th<br>1670 Fulton St<br>Brooklyn, NY 11213<br>**T:**7187745882<br>**F:**7187745730 | **Anthony Weiner** 9th<br>1800 Sheepshead Bay Rd<br>Brooklyn, NY 11235<br>**T:**7187430441<br>**F:**7185209010 |
| **Jim Walsh** 25th<br>1180 Canandalgua Rd<br>Palmyra, NY 14522<br>**T:**3155976138<br>**F:**3155976631 | **North Carolina**<br>**G K Butterfield** 1st<br>415 E Blvd<br>Ste 100<br>Williamton, NC 27892<br>**T:**2527894939<br>**F:**2527928113 |
| **Howard Coble** 6th<br>1634 North Main St<br>Ste 101<br>High Point, NC 27262<br>**T:**3368865106<br>**F:**3368868740 | **Bob Etheridge** 2nd<br>225 Hillsborough St<br>Ste 490<br>Raleigh, NC 27603<br>**T:**9198299122<br>**F:**9198299883 |

| | |
|---|---|
| **Virginia Foxx** 5th<br>240 Hwy 105 Extension<br>Ste 200<br>Boone, NC 28607<br>**T:**8282650240<br>**F:**8282650390 | **Robin Hayes** 8th<br>230 East Franklin St<br>Rockingham, NC 28379<br>**T:**9109972070<br>**F:**9109277987 |
| **Walter Jones** 3rd<br>1105-C Corporate Dr<br>Greenville, NC 27858<br>**T:**2529311003<br>**F:**2529311002 | **Patrick McHenry** 10th<br>311 East Marion St<br>Ste 119<br>Shelby, NC 28050<br>**T:**7044810578<br>**F:**7044810757 |
| **Mike McIntyre** 7th<br>301 Green St<br>Rm 218<br>Fayetteville, NC 28301<br>**T:**9103230260<br>**F:**9103230069 | **Brad Miller** 13th<br>125 S Elm St<br>Ste 504<br>Greensboro, NC 27401<br>**T:**3365742909<br>**F:**3365740607 |
| **Sue Myrick** 9th<br>197 West Main Ave<br>Gastonia, NC 28052<br>**T:**7048611976<br>**F:**7048642445 | **David Price** 4th<br>5400 Trinity Rd<br>Ste 205<br>Raleigh, NC 27607<br>**T:**9198595999<br>**F:**9198595998 |
| **Heather Shuler** 11th<br>356 Biltomore Ave<br>Ste 400<br>Asheville, NC 28801<br>**T:**8282521651<br>**F:**8282528734 | **Mel Watt** 12th<br>1230 W Morehead St<br>Ste 306<br>Charlotte, NC 28208<br>**T:**7043449950<br>**F:**7043449971 |

**North Dakota**
**Earl Pomeroy**
3003 32nd Ave S
Ste 6
Fargo, ND 58103
T:7012359760
F:7012359767

**Ohio**
**John Boehner** 8th
12 South Plum St
Troy, OH 45373
T:9373391524
F:9373391878

**Steve Chabot** 1st
3003 Carew Tower
441 Vine st
Cincinnati, OH 45202
T:5136842723
F:5134218722

**David Hobson** 7th
212 S Broad St
Rm 55
Lancaster, OH 43130
T:7406545149
F:7406547825

**Stephanie Tubbs Jones** 11th
3645 Warrensville Center Rd
Ste 204
Shaker Heights, OH 44122
T:2165224900
F:2165224908

**Jim Jorda** 4th
3121 W Elm Plaza
Lima, OH 45805
T:4199996455
F:4199994238

**Marcy Kaptur** 9th
One Maritime Plaza
6th Flr
Toledo, OH 43604
T:4192597500
F:4192559623

**Dennis Kucinich** 10th
14400 Detroit Ave
Lakewood, OH 44107
T:2162288850
F:2162286465

**Steve LaTourette** 14th
1 Victoria Place
Rm 320
Painesville, OH 44077
T:4403523939
F:4403523622

**Bob Latta** 5th
130 Shady Lane Dr
Norwalk, OH 44857
T:4196680206
F:4196631361

| | |
|---|---|
| **Deborah Pryce** 15th<br>500 S Front St<br>Ste 1130<br>Columbus, OH 43215<br>**T:**6144695614<br>**F:**6144697469 | **Ralph Regula** 16th<br>4150 Belden Village St<br>Ste 408<br>Canton, OH 44718<br>**T:**3304894414<br>**F:**3304894448 |
| **Tim Ryan** 17th<br>1030 Tallmadge Ave<br>Akron, OH 44310<br>**T:**3306307311<br>**F:**3306307314 | **Jean Schmidt** 2nd<br>601 Chillicothe St<br>Portsmouth, OH 45662<br>**T:**7403541440<br>**F:**7403541144 |
| **Zachary Space** 18th<br>137 East Iron Ave<br>Dover, OH 44622<br>**T:**3303644300<br>**F:**3303644330 | **Betty Sutton** 13th<br>1655 West Market<br>Rm 435<br>Akron, OH 44313<br>**T:**3308658450<br>**F:**3308658470 |
| **Pat Tiberi** 12th<br>3000 Corporate Exchange Dr<br>Ste 310<br>Columbus, OH 43231<br>**T:**6145232555<br>**F:**6148180887 | **Michael Turner** 3rd<br>120 West Third St<br>Ste 305<br>Dayton, OH 45402<br>**T:**9372252843<br>**F:**9372252752 |
| **Charles Wilson** 6th<br>258 Front St<br>Marietta, OH 45750<br>**T:**7403760868<br>**F:**7403760886 | **Oklahoma**<br>**Dan Boren** 2nd<br>431 W Broadway<br>Muskogee, OK 74401<br>**T:**9186860128<br>**F:**9186860128 |

| | |
|---|---|
| **Tom Cole** 4th<br>711 SW D Ave<br>Ste 201<br>Lawton, OK 73501<br>**T:**5803577477<br>**F:**5803572131 | **Mary Fallin** 5th<br>120 N Robinson<br>Ste 100<br>Oklahoma City, OK 73102<br>**T:**4052349900<br>**F:**4052349909 |
| **Frank Lucas** 3rd<br>720 South Husband<br>Ste 7<br>Stillwater, OK 74075<br>**T:**4056246407<br>**F:**4056246467 | **John Sullivan** 1st<br>5727 S Lewis Ave<br>Ste 520<br>Tulsa, OK 74105<br>**T:**9187490014<br>**F:**9187490781 |
| **Oregon**<br>**Earl Blumenauer** 3rd<br>729 N.E Oregon St<br>Ste 115<br>Portland, OR 97232<br>**T:**5032312300<br>**F:**5032305413 | **Peter DeFazio** 4th<br>405 E 8th Ave<br># 2030<br>Eugene, OR 97401<br>**T:**5414656732<br>**F:**5414656458 |
| **Darlene Hooley** 5th<br>315 Mission St SE<br># 101<br>Salem, OR 97302<br>**T:**5035889100<br>**F:**5035885517 | **Greg Walden** 2nd<br>843 E Main St<br>Ste 400<br>Medford, OR 97504<br>**T:**5413894408<br>**F:**5417790204 |
| **David Wu** 1st<br>620 SW Main<br>Ste 606<br>Portland, OR 97205<br>**T:**5033262901<br>**F:**5033265066 | **Pennsylvania**<br>**Jason Altmire** 4th<br>2110 McLean St<br>Alquippa, PA 15001<br>**T:**7243780928<br>**F:**7243786171 |

| | |
|---|---|
| **Robert Brady** 1st<br>1907-09 S Broad St<br>Philadelphia, PA 19148<br>**T:**2153894627<br>**F:**2153894636 | **Christopher Carney** 10th<br>233 Northern Blvd<br>Ste 4<br>Clarks Summit, PA 18411<br>**T:**5705859988<br>**F:**5705859977 |
| **Charles Dent** 15th<br>701 W Broad St<br>Ste 200<br>Bethlehem, PA 18018<br>**T:**6108619734<br>**F:**6108612624 | **Mike Doyle** 14th<br>225 Ross St<br>Fifth Flr<br>Pittsburg, PA 15219<br>**T:**4122615091<br>**F:**4122611983 |
| **Phil English** 3rd<br>749 Greenville Rd<br>Ste 200<br>Mercer, PA 16137<br>**T:**7246623222<br>**F:**7246622796 | **Chaka Fattah** 2nd<br>4104 Walnut St<br>Philadelphia, PA 19119<br>**T:**2153876404<br>**F:**2153876407 |
| **Jim Gerlach** 6th<br>111 E Uwchlan Ave<br>Exton, PA 19341<br>**T:**6105941415<br>**F:**6105941419 | **Paul Kanjorski** 11th<br>548 Spruce St<br>Scranton, PA 18503<br>**T:**5704961011<br>**F:**5704966439 |
| **Tim Holden** 17th<br>4918 Kutztown Rd<br>Temple, PA 19560<br>**T:**6109213502<br>**F:**6109213504 | **Patrick Murphy** 8th<br>414 Mill St<br>Bristol, PA 19007<br>**T:**2158261963<br>**F:**2158261997 |

**Tim Murphy** 18th
504 Washington Rd
Pittsburg, PA 15228
**T:**4122445583
**F:**4124295092

**John Murtha** 12th
647 Main St
Ste 401
Johnstown, PA 15901
**T:**8145352642
**F:**8145396229

**Joe Pitts** 16th
50 North Duke St
Lancaster, PA 17602
**T:**7173930667
**F:**7173930924

**Todd Platts** 19th
22 Chamberburg St
Gettysburg, PA 17325
**T:**7173381919
**F:**7133346314

**Allyson Schwartz** 13th
706 West Ave
Jenkintown, PA 19046
**T:**2155176572
**F:**2155176575

**Joe Sestak** 7th
600 N Jackson St
Ste 203
Media, PA 19063
**T:**6108928623
**F:**6108928628

**Bill Shuster** 9th
310 Penn St
Ste 200
Hollidaysburg, PA 16648
**T:**8146966318
**F:**81469866726

**Rhode Island**
**Patrick Kennedy** 1st
249 Roosevelt Ave
Ste 200
Pawtucket, RI 02860
**T:**4017295600
**F:**4017295608

**Jim Langevin** 2nd
300 Centerville Rd
Ste 200 South
Warwick, RI 02886
**T:**4017329400
**F:**4017372982

**South Carolina**
**J. Gresham Barrett** 3rd
303 West Beltline Blvd
Anderson, SC 29625
**T:**8642247401
**F:**8642257049

| | |
|---|---|
| **Henry Brown** 1st<br>5900 Core Ave<br>Ste 401<br>North Charleston, SC 29406<br>**T:**8437474175<br>**F:**8437474711 | **James Clyburn** 6th<br>1225 Lady St<br>Ste 200<br>Columbia, SC 29506<br>**T:**8037991100<br>**F:**8037999060 |
| **Bob Inglis** 4th<br>105 N Spring St<br>Ste 111<br>Greenville, SC 29601<br>**T:**8642321141<br>**F:**8642332160 | **John Spratt** 5th<br>201 E Main St<br>Ste 305<br>Rock Hill, SC 29730<br>**T:**8037733362<br>**F:**8037737662 |
| **Joe Wilson** 2nd<br>1700 Sunset Blvd (US 378)<br>Ste 1<br>West Columbia, SC 29169<br>**T:**8039390041<br>**F:**8039390078 | South Dakota<br>**Stephanie Herseth Sandlin**<br>326 E 8th St<br>Ste 108<br>Sioux Falls, SD 57104<br>**T:**6053678371<br>**F:**6053678373 |
| Tennessee<br>**Marsha Blackburn** 7th<br>1850 Memorial Dr<br>Clarksville, TN 37043<br>**T:**9315030391<br>**F:**9315030393 | **Steve Cohen** 9th<br>167 N. Main St<br>Ste 369<br>Memphis, TN 38103<br>**T:**9015444131<br>**F:**9015444329 |
| **Jim Cooper** 5th<br>605 Church St<br>Nashville, TN 37219<br>**T:**6157365295<br>**F:**6157367479 | **David Davis** 1st<br>2425 Highway 75<br>Blountville, TN 37617<br>**T:**4233231235<br>**F:**4233231972 |

**Lincoln Davis** 4th
1804 Carmack Blvd
Ste A
Columbia, TN 38401
**T:**9318792361
**F:**9314908675

**John Duncun Jr** 2nd
200 E Broadway Ave
Ste 414
Maryville, TN 37804
**T:**8659845464
**F:**8659840521

**Bart Gordon** 6th
305 West Main St
Murfreesboro, TN 37130
**T:**6158961986
**F:**6158968218

**John Tanner** 8th
PO Box 629
Union City, TN 38281
**T:**7318857070
**F:**7314271537

**Zach Wamp** 3rd
900 Georgia Ave
Ste 126
Chattanooga, TN 37402
**T:**4237562342
**F:**4237656613

**Texas**
**Joe Barton** 6th
6001 West Ronald Regan
Memorial Hwy Ste 200
Arlington, TX 76017
**T:**8175431000
**F:**8175487029

**Kevin Brady** 8th
200 River Pointe
Ste 304
Conroe, TX 77304
**T:**9364415700
**F:**9364415757

**Michael Burgess** 26th
1660 South Stemmons Fwy
Ste 230
Lewisville, TX 75067
**T:**9724349700
**F:**9724349705

**John Carter** 31st
1717 North IH 35
Ste 303
Round Rock, TX 78664
**T:**5122461600
**F:**5122461620

**Michael Conaway** 11th
411 W 8th St
5th Flr
Odessa, TX 79761
**T:**4323319667
**F:**4323326538

| | |
|---|---|
| **Henry Cuellar** 28th<br>602 E Calton Rd<br>Ste 2<br>Laredo, TX 78041<br>**T:**9567250639<br>**F:**9567252647 | **John Culberson** 7th<br>10000 Memorial Dr<br>Ste 620<br>Houston, TX 77024<br>**T:**7136828828<br>**F:**7136808070 |
| **Lloyd Doggett** 25th<br>300 E 8th St<br>#763<br>Austin, TX 78701<br>**T:**5129165921<br>**F:**5129165108 | **Chet Edwards** 17th<br>600 Austin Ave<br>Ste 29<br>Waco, TX 76701<br>**T:**2547529600<br>**F:**2547527769 |
| **Louie Gohmert** 1st<br>101 E Methvin<br>Ste 302<br>Longview, TX 75601<br>**T:**9032368597<br>**F:**9035617110 | **Charlie Gonzalez** 20th<br>B-124 Federal Bldg<br>727 E Durango<br>San Antonio, TX 78206<br>**T:**2104726195<br>**F:**2104724009 |
| **Kay Granger** 12th<br>1701 River Run Rd<br>Ste 07<br>Fort Worth, TX 76107<br>**T:**8173380909<br>**F:**8172255852 | **Al Green** 9th<br>3003 South Loop West<br>Ste 460<br>Houston, TX 77054<br>**T:**7133839234<br>**F:**7133839202 |
| **Gene Green** 29th<br>256 N Sam Houston Pkwy E<br>Ste 29<br>Houston, TX 77060<br>**T:**2819995879<br>**F:**2819995716 | **Ralph Hall** 4th<br>104 N San Jacinto St<br>Rockwall, TX 75087<br>**T:**9727719118<br>**F:**9727220907 |

| | |
|---|---|
| **Jeb Hensarling** 5th<br>702 E Corsicana St<br>Athens, TX 75751<br>**T:**9036758288<br>**F:**9036758351 | **Ruben Hinojosa** 15th<br>2864 West Trenton Rd<br>Edinburg, TX 78539<br>**T:**9566825545<br>**F:**9566820141 |
| **Shelia Jackson Lee** 18th<br>1919 Smith St<br>Ste 1180<br>Houston, TX 77002<br>**T:**7136550050<br>**F:**7136551612 | **Eddie Bernice Johnson**<br>30th<br>3102 Maple Ave<br>Ste 600<br>Dallas, TX 75201<br>**T:**2149228885<br>**F:**2149227028 |
| **Sam Johnson** 3rd<br>2929 North Central Expressway<br>Ste 240<br>Richardson, TX 76080<br>**T:**9724700892<br>**F:**9724709937 | **Nick Lampson** 22nd<br>10701 Corporate Dr<br>Ste 118<br>Stafford, TX 77477<br>**T:**2812403700<br>**F:**2812402959 |
| **Kenny Marchant** 24th<br>9901 E Valley Ranch Pkwy<br>Ste 3035<br>Irving, TX 75063<br>**T:**9725560162<br>**F:**9724099704 | **Michael McCaul** 10th<br>5929 Balcones Dr<br>Ste 305<br>Austin, TX 78731<br>**T:**5124732357<br>**F:**5124730514 |
| **Randy Neugebauer** 19th<br>508 Chestnut St<br>Ste 819<br>Abilene, TX 79602<br>**T:**3256759779<br>**F:**3256755038 | **Solomon Ortiz** 27th<br>3649 Leopard<br>Corpus Christi, TX 78408<br>**T:**3618835868<br>**F:**3618849201 |

| | |
|---|---|
| **Ron Paul** 14th<br>122 West Way<br>Ste 301<br>Lake Jackson, TX 77566<br>**T:**9792850231<br>**F:**9792850271 | **Ted Poe** 2nd<br>20202 US Hwy 59 N<br>Ste 105<br>Humble, TX 77338<br>**T:**2814460242<br>**F:**2814460242 |
| **Silvestre Reyes** 16th<br>310 N Mesa<br>Ste 400<br>El Paso, TX 79901<br>**T:**9155344400<br>**F:**9155347426 | **Ciro Rodriguez** 23rd<br>1995 Williams St<br>Ste B<br>Eagle Pass, TX 78852<br>**T:**8307571893<br>**F:**8307521893 |
| **Pete Sessions** 32nd<br>12750 Merit Dr<br>Ste 1434<br>Dallas, TX 75251<br>**T:**9723920505<br>**F:**9723920615 | **Lamar Smith** 21st<br>3536 Bee Cave Rd<br>Ste 212<br>Austin, TX 78746<br>**T:**5123060439<br>**F:**5123060427 |
| **Mac Thornberry** 13th<br>905 S Fillmore St<br>Ste 520<br>Amarillo, TX 79101<br>**T:**8063718844<br>**F:**8063717044 | **Utah**<br>**Rob Bishop** 1st<br>125 South State St<br>Ste 5420<br>Salt Lake City, UT 84302<br>**T:**8016250107<br>**F:**8016250124 |
| **Chris Cannon** 3rd<br>51 S University Ave<br>Ste 319<br>Provo, UT 84601<br>**T:**8018512500<br>**F:**8018512509 | **Jim Matheson** 2nd<br>240 E Morris Ave<br># 235<br>South Salt Lake, UT 84115<br>**T:**8014861236<br>**F:**8014861417 |

| | |
|---|---|
| **Vermont**<br>**Peter Welch**<br>30 Main St<br>Third Flr Ste 350<br>Burlington, VT 05401<br>**T:**8886057270<br>**F:**8026522450 | **Virginia**<br>**Eric Cantor** 7th<br>4201 Dominion Blvd<br>Ste 110<br>Glen Allen, VA 23060<br>**T:**8047474073<br>**F:**8047475308 |
| **Rick Boucher** 9th<br>188 E Main St<br>Abingdon, VA 24210<br>**T:**2766281145<br>**F:** | **Thelma Drake** 2nd<br>4772 Euclid Rd<br>Ste E<br>Virginia Beach, VA 23462<br>**T:**7574976859<br>**F:**7574975474 |
| **Tom Davis** 11th<br>4115 Annadale Rd<br>Ste 103<br>Annadale, VA 22003<br>**T:**7039169610<br>**F:**7039168617 | **Virgil Goode** 5th<br>437 Main St<br>Danville, VA 24541<br>**T:**4347921280<br>**F:**4347975942 |
| **Randy Forbes** 4th<br>505 Independence Pkwy<br>Ste 104<br>Chesapeake, VA 23320<br>**T:**7573820080<br>**F:**7573820780 | **Jim Moran** 8th<br>333 N Fairfax St<br>Ste 201<br>Alexandria, VA 22314<br>**T:**7039714700<br>**F:**7039229436 |
| **Bobby Scott** 3rd<br>2600 Washington Ave<br>Ste 1010<br>Newport News, VA 23607<br>**T:**7573801000<br>**F:**7579286694 | **Robert Wittman** 1st<br>12000 Kennedy Ln<br>Ste 106<br>Fredericksburg, VA 22407<br>**T:**5405481086<br>**F:** |

**Frank Wolf** 10th
13873 Park Center Rd
Ste 130
Herndon, VA 20171
**T:**7037095800
**F:**7037095802

**Brian Baird** 3rd
120 Union Ave
Ste 105
Olympia, WA 98501
**T:**3603529768
**F:**3603529241

**Norman Dicks** 6th
1019 Pacific Ave
Ste 806
Tacoma, WA 98402
**T:**2535936536
**F:**2535936551

**Doc Hasting** 4th
2715 St Andrews Loop
Ste D
Pasco, WA 99301
**T:**5095439396
**F:**5095451972

**Jay Inslee** 1st
18560 1st Ave NE
Ste E-800
Shoreline, WA 98155
**T:**2063610233
**F:**2063613959

**Rick Larsen** 2nd
104 W Magnolia
Rm 206
Bellingham, WA 98225
**T:**3607334500
**F:**3607335144

**Jim McDermott** 7th
1809 7th Ave
Ste 1212
Seattle, WA 98101
**T:**2065537170
**F:**2065337175

**Cathy McMorris Rodgers** 5th
10 North Post
6th Flr
Spokane, WA 99201
**T:**5093532412
**F:**5093532412

**David Reichert** 8th
2737 78th Ave SE
Ste 202 2nd Flr
Mercer Island, WA 98040
**T:**2062753438
**F:**2062753437

**Adam Smith** 9th
3600 Port of Tacoma Rd
Ste 106
Tacoma, WA 98424
**T:**2538963775
**F:**2538963789

**Wisconsin**

**Tammy Baldwin**
10 E Doty St
Ste 405
Madison, WI 53703
T:6083622800
F:6082589808

**Steve Kagen** 8th
700 E Walnut ST
Green Bay, WI 54301
T:9204371954
F:9204371978

**Ron Kind** 3rd
205 Fifth Ave S
Ste 400
LaCrosse, WI 54601
T:6087822558
F:6087824588

**Gwen Moore** 4th
219 N Milwaukee St
Ste 3A
Milwaukee, WI 53202
T:4142971140
F:4142971086

**Dave Obey** 7th
401 5th St
Ste 406A
Wausau, WI 54403
T:7158425606
F:7158424488

**Thomas Petri** 6th
2390 State Rd 44
Ste B
Oshkosh, WI 54904
T:9209221180
F:9209224498

**Paul Ryan** 1st
20 South Main St
Ste 10
Janesville, WI 53545
T:6087524050
F:6087524711

**West Virginia**

**Shelley Moore Capito** 2nd
300 Foxcroft Ave
Ste 102
Martinsburg, WV 25401
T:3042648810
F:3042648815

**Alan Mollohan** 1st
Room 209 POB
PO Box 1400
Clarksburg, WV 26302
T:3046234422
F:3046230571

**Nick Rahall** 3rd
301 Prince St
Beckley, WV 25801
T:3042525000
F:

**Wyoming**
## Barbara Cubin
100 East B St
Ste 4003
Casper, WY 82601
**T:**3072616595
**F:**3072616597

# Senate

| | |
|---|---|
| **Lisa Murkowski**<br>110 Trading Bay Rd<br>Ste 105<br>Kenai, AK 99611<br>**T:**9072835808<br>**F:**9072834363 | **Ted Stevens**<br>222 West 7th Ave<br>Ste 2<br>Anchorage, AK 99501<br>**T:**9072715915<br>**F:**9072589305 |
| **Jeff Sessions**<br>1800 5th Ave North<br>341 Vance Federal Bldg<br>Birmingham, AL 35203<br>**T:**2057311500<br>**F:**2057310221 | **Richard Shelby**<br>113 St. Joseph St<br>445 US Federal Courthouse<br>Mobile, AL 36602<br>**T:**2516944164<br>**F:**2516944166 |
| **Blanche Lincoln**<br>912 West Fourth St<br>Little Rock, AR 72201<br>**T:**5013752993<br>**F:**5013757064 | **Mark Pryor**<br>500 Clinton Ave<br>Ste 401<br>Little Rock, AR 72201<br>**T:**5013246336<br>**F:**5013245320 |

| | |
|---|---|
| **Jon Kyl**<br>2200 East Camelback<br>Ste 120<br>Phoenix, AZ 85016<br>**T:**6028401891<br>**F:**6029576838 | **John McCain**<br>5353 North 16th St<br>Ste 105<br>Phoenix, AZ 85016<br>**T:**6029522410<br>**F:**6029528702 |
| **Barbara Boxer**<br>1700 Montgomery St<br>Ste 240<br>San Francisco, CA 94111<br>**T:**4154030100<br>**F:**2022240454 | **Dianne Feinstein**<br>One Post Street<br>Ste 2450<br>San Francisco, CA 94101<br>**T:**4153930707<br>**F:**4153930710 |
| **Wayne Allard**<br>7340 E Caley<br>Ste 215<br>Englewood, CO 80111<br>**T:**3032207414<br>**F:**3032208126 | **Kay Salazar**<br>2300 15th St<br>Ste 450<br>Denver, CO 80202<br>**T:**3034557600<br>**F:**3034558851 |
| **Chris Dodd**<br>30 Lewis St<br>Ste 101<br>Hartford, CT 06103<br>**T:**8602586940<br>**F:**8602586958 | **Joe Liberman**<br>One Constitution Plaza<br>7th Flr<br>Hartford, CT 06103<br>**T:**8605498463<br>**F:**8605498478 |
| **Joseph Biden Jr**<br>24 NW Front St<br>Windsor Bldg Ste 101<br>Milford, DE 19963<br>**T:**3024248090<br>**F:**3024248094 | **Thomas Carper**<br>12 The Circle<br>Georgetown, DE 19947<br>**T:**3028567690<br>**F:**3028563001 |

| | |
|---|---|
| **Mel Martinez**<br>T:4072542573<br>F:4074230941 | **Bill Nelson**<br>2925 Salzedo St<br>Coral Gables, FL 33134<br>T:3055365999<br>F:3055365991 |
| **Saxby Chambliss**<br>100 Galleria Pkwy<br>Ste 1340<br>Atlanta, GA 30339<br>T:7707639090<br>F:7702268633 | **Johnny Isakson**<br>One Overton Park Ste 970<br>3625 Cumberland Blvd<br>Atlanta, GA 30339<br>T:7706610999<br>F:7706610768 |
| **Daniel Akaka**<br>101 Aupuni St<br>Ste 213<br>Hilo, HA 96720<br>T:8089351114<br>F:8089359064 | **Daniel Inouye**<br>101 Aupuni St<br>Ste 205<br>Hilo, HA 96720<br>T:8089350844<br>F:8089615163 |
| **Chuck Grassley**<br>206 Federal Bldg<br>101 1st St SE<br>Cedar Rapids, IA 52401<br>T:3193636832<br>F:3193637179 | **Tom Harkin**<br>1606 Brady St<br>Ste 323<br>Davenport, IA 52803<br>T:5633221338<br>F:5633220417 |
| **Larry Craig**<br>225 North 9th St<br>Ste 530<br>Boise, ID 83702<br>T:2083427985<br>F:2023482458 | **Mike Crapo**<br>490 Memorial Dr<br>Ste 102<br>Idaho Falls, ID 83402<br>T:2085229779<br>F:2025298367 |

| | |
|---|---|
| **Dirk Durbin**<br>230 S Dearborn St<br>Ste 3892<br>Chicago, IL 60604<br>**T:**3123534952<br>**F:**3123530150 | **Barack Obama**<br>607 East Adams St<br>Springfield, IL 62701<br>**T:**2174925089<br>**F:**2174925099 |
| **Evan Bayh**<br>101 MLK Jr Blvd<br>Evansville, IN 47708<br>**T:**8124656500<br>**F:**8124656503 | **Richard Lugar**<br>101 MLK Jr Blvd<br>Ste 122<br>Evansville, IN 47708<br>**T:**8124656313<br>**F:**8124211883 |
| **Sam Brownback**<br>245 N. Waco<br>Ste 240<br>Wichita, KS 67202<br>**T:**31626482066<br>**F:**3162649078 | **Pat Roberts**<br>11900 College Blvd<br>Ste 203<br>Overland Park, KS 66210<br>**T:**9134519343<br>**F:**9134519446 |
| **Jim Bunning**<br>1717 Dixie Hwy<br>Ste 220<br>Ft. Wright, KY 41011<br>**T:**8593412602<br>**F:**8593317445 | **Mitch McConnell**<br>241 E. Main St<br>Room 102<br>Bowling Green, KY 42101<br>**T:**2707811673<br>**F:** |
| **Mary Landrieu**<br>500 Poydras St<br>Room 1005<br>New Orleans, LA 70130<br>**T:**5045892427<br>**F:**5045894023 | **David Vitter**<br>858 Convention St<br>Baton Rouge, LA 70802<br>**T:**2253830331<br>**F:**2253830952 |

| | |
|---|---|
| **Edward Kennedy**<br>2400 JFK Bldg<br>Boston, MA 02203<br>**T:**6175653170<br>**F:**6175653183 | **John Kerry**<br>1550 Main St<br>Ste 304<br>Springfield, MA 01101<br>**T:**413785460<br>**F:**4137361049 |
| **Benjamin Cardin**<br>Tower 1 Ste. 1710<br>100 South Charles St<br>Baltimore, MD 21201<br>**T:**4109624436<br>**F:**4109624156 | **Barbara Mikulski**<br>60 West St<br>Ste 202<br>Annapolis, MD 21401<br>**T:**4102631805<br>**F:**4102635949 |
| **Susan Collins**<br>One City Center<br>Ste 23<br>Portland, ME 04101<br>**T:**2077803575<br>**F:** | **Olympia Snowe**<br>3 Canal Plaza<br>Ste 601<br>Portland, ME 04101<br>**T:**2078740883<br>**F:**2078747631 |
| **Carl Levin**<br>477 Michigan Ave<br>Room 1860<br>Detroit, MI 48226<br>**T:**3132266020<br>**F:**3132266948 | **Debbie Stabenow**<br>3280 Beltline Ct<br>Ste 400<br>Grand Rapids, MI 49525<br>**T:**6169750052<br>**F:** |
| **Norm Coleman**<br>2550 University Ave<br>Ste 100N<br>St. Paul, MN 55114<br>**T:**6516450323<br>**F:**6516453110 | **Amy Klobuchar**<br>1134 7th St NW<br>Rochester, MN 55901<br>**T:**5072285321<br>**F:**5072282922 |

| | |
|---|---|
| **Chistopher Bond**<br>308 East High<br>Ste 202<br>Jefferson City, MO 64105<br>**T:**5736342488<br>**F:** | **Claire McCaskill**<br>400 East 9th St<br>Ste 40 Plaza Level<br>Kansas City, MO 64106<br>**T:**8164211639<br>**F:**8164212562 |
| **Thad Cochran**<br>188 East Capitol St<br>Ste 614<br>Jackson, MS 39201<br>**T:**6019654459<br>**F:** | **Roger Wicker**<br>**T:**6019654644<br>**F:**6019654007 |
| **Max Baucus**<br>222 N 32nd St<br>Ste 100<br>Billings, MT 59101<br>**T:**4066576790<br>**F:** | **Jon Tester**<br>119 1st Avenue North<br>Ste 102<br>Great Falls, MT 59401<br>**T:**4064529585<br>**F:**4064529586 |
| **Richard Burr**<br>2000 West First St<br>Ste 508<br>Winston-Salem, NC 27104<br>**T:**3366315125<br>**F:**3367254493 | **Elizabeth Dole**<br>310 New Bern Ave<br>Ste 122<br>Raleigh, NC 27601<br>**T:**9198564630<br>**F:**9198564053 |
| **Kent Conrad**<br>US Federal Bldg Rm 105<br>1001 1st St SW<br>Minot, ND 58701<br>**T:**7018520703<br>**F:** | **Byron Dorgan**<br>1802 32nd Ave South Ste. B<br>PO Box 9060<br>Fargo, ND 58106<br>**T:**7012395389<br>**F:**7012395112 |

| | |
|---|---|
| **Chuck Hagel**<br>9900 Nicholas St<br>Ste 325<br>Omaha, NE 68114<br>**T:**4027588981<br>**F:**4027589165 | **Ben Nelson**<br>7602 Pacific St<br>Ste 205<br>Omaha, NE 68114<br>**T:**4023913411<br>**F:**4023914725 |
| **Judd Gregg**<br>41 Hooksett Rd<br>Manchester, NH 03104<br>**T:**6036227979<br>**F:** | **John Sununu**<br>60 Pleasant St<br>Berlin, NH 03570<br>**T:**6037526074<br>**F:**6037526423 |
| **Frank Lautenberg**<br>One Gateway Center<br>Twenty-Third Flr<br>Newark, NJ 07102<br>**T:**9736398700<br>**F:**9736398723 | **Robert Menedez**<br>One Gateway Center<br>Ste 1100<br>Newark, NJ 07102<br>**T:**9736453030<br>**F:**9736450502 |
| **Jeff Bingaman**<br>625 Silver Ave SW<br>Albuquerque, NM 87102<br>**T:**5053466601<br>**F:** | **Pete Domenici**<br>140 Federal Bldg<br>Roswell, NM 88201<br>**T:**5056236170<br>**F:**5056252547 |
| **John Ensign**<br>333 Las Vegas Blvd S<br>Ste 8203<br>Las Vegas, NV 89101<br>**T:**7023886605<br>**F:**7023886501 | **Harry Reid**<br>333 Las Vegas Blvd S<br>Ste 8016<br>Las Vegas, NV 89101<br>**T:**7023885020<br>**F:**7703885030 |
| **Hillary Clinton**<br>780 Third Ave<br>Ste 2601<br>New York, NY 10017<br>**T:**2126886262<br>**F:**2126887444 | **Charles Schumer**<br>757 Third Ave<br>Ste 17-02<br>New York, NY 10017<br>**T:**2124864430<br>**F:**2124867693 |

| | |
|---|---|
| **Sherrod Brown**<br>1301 E 9th ST<br>Ste 1710<br>Cleveland, OH 44114<br>**T:**2165227272<br>**F:**2165222239 | **George Vornovich**<br>1240 E. 9th St<br>Rm 3061<br>Cleveland, OH 44199<br>**T:**2165227095<br>**F:**2165227097 |
| **Tom Coburn**<br>1800 South Baltimore<br>Ste 800<br>Tulsa, OK 74119<br>**T:**9185817651<br>**F:**9185817195 | **James Inhoe**<br>1924 S. Utica Ave<br>Ste. 530<br>Tulsa, OK 74101<br>**T:**9187485111<br>**F:**9187485119 |
| **Gordon Smith**<br>Jager Bldg<br>116 South Main St Ste 3<br>Pendleton, OR 97801<br>**T:**5412781129<br>**F:**5412784109 | **Ron Wyden**<br>405 E 8th Ave<br>Ste 2020<br>Eugene, OR 97401<br>**T:**5414310229<br>**F:** |
| **Robert Casey Jr**<br>2000 Market St<br>Ste 1870<br>Philadelphia, PA 19106<br>**T:**2154059660<br>**F:**2154059669 | **Arlen Specter**<br>600 Arch St<br>Ste 9400<br>Philadelphia, PA 19106<br>**T:**2155977200<br>**F:**2155970406 |
| **Jack Reed**<br>1000 Chapel View Blvd<br>Ste 290<br>Cranston, RI 02920<br>**T:**4019433100<br>**F:**4014646837 | **Sheldon Whitehouse**<br>170 Westminister St<br>St 1100<br>Providence, RI 02903<br>**T:**4014535294<br>**F:**4014535085 |

| | |
|---|---|
| **Jim DeMint**<br>1901 Main St<br>Ste 1475<br>Columbia, SC 29201<br>**T:**8037716112<br>**F:**8037716455 | **Lindsey Graham**<br>508 Hampton St<br>Ste 202<br>Columbia, SC 29201<br>**T:**8033930112<br>**F:** |
| **Tim Johnson**<br>405 E. Omaha St<br>Ste B<br>Rapid City, SD 57701<br>**T:**6053413990<br>**F:**6053412207 | **John Thune**<br>1313 West Main St<br>Rapid City, SD 57701<br>**T:**6053487551<br>**F:** |
| **Lamar Alexander**<br>3322 West End Ave<br>#120<br>Nashville, TN 37203<br>**T:**6157365129<br>**F:**6152694803 | **Bob Corker**<br>10 West MLK Blvd<br>6th Flr<br>Chattanooga, TN 37402<br>**T:**4237562757<br>**F:**4237565315 |
| **John Cornyn**<br>5300 Memorial Dr<br>Ste 980<br>Houston, TX 77007<br>**T:**7135723337<br>**F:**7135723777 | **Kay Bailey Hutchinson**<br>145 Duncan Dr<br>Ste 120<br>San Antonio, TX 78226<br>**T:**2103402885<br>**F:**2103496753 |
| **Bob Bennett**<br>125 South State ST<br>Ste 4225<br>Salt Lake City, UT 84101<br>**T:**8015245933<br>**F:**8015245730 | **Orrin Hatch**<br>51 S. University Ave<br>Ste 320<br>Provo, UT 84606<br>**T:**80137578818<br>**F:**8013745005 |

| | |
|---|---|
| **John Warner**<br>101 W. Main St<br>Ste 4900<br>Norfolk, VA 23510<br>**T:**7574413079<br>**F:**7574416250 | **Jim Webb**<br>222 Central Park Ave<br>Ste 120<br>Virginia Beach, VA 23462<br>**T:**7575181674<br>**F:**7575181679 |
| **Patrick Leahy**<br>199 Main St<br>4th Flr<br>Burlington, VT 05401<br>**T:**8028632525<br>**F:** | **Bernard Sanders**<br>1 Church ST<br>2nd Flr<br>Burlington, VT 05401<br>**T:**8028620697<br>**F:**8028606370 |
| **Maria Cantwell**<br>915 Second Ave<br>Ste 3206<br>Seattle, WA 98174<br>**T:**2062206400<br>**F:**2062206404 | **Patty Murray**<br>950 Pacific Ave<br>Ste 650<br>Tacoma, WA 98402<br>**T:**2535723636<br>**F:**2535729882 |
| **Russell Feingood**<br>1600 Aspen Commons<br>Middleton, WI 53562<br>**T:**6088281200<br>**F:**6088281203 | **Herb Kohl**<br>310 West Wisconsin Ave<br>Ste 950<br>Milwaukee, WI 53203<br>**T:**4142974451<br>**F:**4142974455 |
| **Robert Byrd**<br>300 Virginia St East<br>Ste 2630<br>Charleston, WV 25301<br>**T:**3043425855<br>**F:** | **Jay Rockefeller**<br>220 North Kanawha St<br>Ste 1<br>Beckley, WV 25801<br>**T:**3042539704<br>**F:**3042532578 |

| John Barrasso | Mike Enzi |
|---|---|
| 100 East B st | 400 S. Kendrick Ave |
| Ste 2201 | Ste 303 |
| Casper, WY 82602 | Gillette, WY 82716 |
| **T:**3072616413 | **T:**3076826268 |
| **F:** | **F:**3076826501 |

# References

1. Center on Budget and Policy Priorities, *The Number of Uninsured is at an All-Time High*, Washington, DC: Center on Budget and Policy Priorities, Aug. 2006.

2. U.S. Department of Defense, Office of the Assistant Secretary of Defense (Public Affairs). "DoD Identifies Casualties," News Release, 11 Jan. 2008.

3. The Henry J. Kaiser Family Foundation, *The Uninsured: A Primer, Key Facts About Americans without Health Insurance*, Menlo Park California: The Henry J. Kaiser Family Foundation, Oct. 2007.

4. Center on Budget and Policy Priorities, *The Number of Uninsured is at an All-Time High*, Washington, DC: Center on Budget and Policy Priorities, Aug. 2006.

5. The Association of Faculties of Medicine of Canada, *Admission Requirements of Canadian Faculties of Medicine, Admission in 2008*, Ottawa, OH: The Association of Faculties of Medicine of Canada, 2008.

6. Rishi Manchanda, "Treating the Poor: A Gap in Doctor Training," <u>*Los Angeles Times,*</u> 9 April 2007.

7. American Medical Association, *An Environmental Analysis Report: Healthcare Trends 2006*, Chicago, Illinois: American Medical Association, 2006.

8. Centers for Disease Control and Prevention, *Working Together to Manage Diabetes: A Guide for Pharmacists, Podiatrists, Optometrists, and Dental Professionals*, Atlanta, Georgia: U.S. Department of Health and Human Services, Public Health Service, Centers for Disease Control and Prevention, National Center for Chronic Disease Prevention and Health Promotion, 2007.

9. Merritt Hawkins & Associates ®, *2007 Survey of Primary Care Physicians*, Irving, Texas: Merritt Hawkins & Associates, 2007.

10. Ruth, Erin. (2006), *Health Care Financing and Reimbursement.*

11. Association of American Medical Colleges. *Help Wanted: More U.S. Doctors Projections Indicate America Will Face Shortage of M.D.s by 2020*, Washington DC: Association of American Medical Colleges, 2006.

12. Reuters, "Roche sues Dr Reddy's in US over generic bone drug," Sep 25, 2007.

13. Centers for Disease Control and Prevention, 2008.

14. DeWaal Smith, Caroline. Testimony. Center for Science in the Public Interest. H.R. 3610, The Food and Drub Import Safety Act. 26 Sept. 2007.

15. Council on Graduate Medical Education. Sixteenth Report: *COGME Physician Workforce Policy Guidelines for the United States, 2000-2020*. Rockville, MD. Department of Health and Human Services, Human Resources Services Administration, 2005.

16. Cauchon, Dennis, "Doctor Shortage a Concern," *USA Today*, 2 March 2005.

17. American Medical Association. International Medical Graduates in the U.S. Workforce Discussion Paper. Chicago, Illinois: American Medical Association, 2006.

18. Association of American Medical Colleges. Help Wanted: More U.S. Doctors Projections Indicate America Will Face Shortage of M.D.s by 2020. Washington DC: Association of American Medical Colleges; 2006.

19. Association of American Medical Colleges. Help Wanted: More U.S. Doctors Projections Indicate America Will Face Shortage of M.D.s by 2020. Washington DC: Association of American Medical Colleges; 2006.

20. Association of American Medical Colleges. Help Wanted: More U.S. Doctors Projections Indicate America Will Face Shortage of M.D.s by 2020. Washington DC: Association of American Medical Colleges; 2006.

21. Association of American Medical Colleges. Help Wanted: More U.S. Doctors Projections Indicate America Will Face Shortage of M.D.s by 2020. Washington DC: Association of American Medical Colleges; 2006.

22. Association of American Medical Colleges. Help Wanted: More U.S. Doctors Projections Indicate America Will Face Shortage of M.D.s by 2020. Washington DC: Association of American Medical Colleges; 2006.

23. Foundation for Advancement of International Medical Education and Research, Mapping the World's Medical Schools, Philadelphia, PA; Foundation for Advancement of International Medical Education and Research; 2007. Website: www.faimer.org/resources/mapping.html.

24. Association of American Medical Colleges. Help Wanted: More U.S. Doctors Projections Indicate America Will Face Shortage of M.D.s by 2020. Washington DC: Association of American Medical Colleges; 2006.

25. Bureau of Labor Statistics, U.S. Department of Labor, *Occupational Outlook Handbook, 2008-09 Edition*, Physician Assistants, on the Internet at **http://www.bls.gov/oco/ocos081.htm** (visited January 28, 2008).

26. American Medical Association, Collegiate Funding Services, Medical Education Financing and Debt Management, Fredericksburg, Virginia: American Medical Association; 2005.

27. Central European and Eurasian Law Initiative (CEELI), Law School Accreditation in the New Independent States of the Former Soviet Union: What Steps for the Future, Washington, DC: Central European and Eurasian Law Initiative; 2003.

28. Baicker, Katherine and Chandra, Amitbh. "The Productivity of Physician Specialization: Evidence from the Medicare Program." May 2004.

29. National Institutes of Health, Health Disparities, Washington DC: National Institutes of Health; October 2006.

30. Association of American Medical Colleges, Minorities in Medical Education, Facts and Figure, Washington DC: Association of American Medical Colleges; 2005.

31. Council on Graduate Medical Education. Twelfth Report: Minorities in Medicine. Rockville, MD: Department of Health and Human Services, Health Resources and Services Administration; 1998.

32. Citizens' Health Care Working Group. The Health Report to the American People, Bethesda, Maryland: Citizens' Health Care Working Group; 2006 and Deloitte Center for Health Solutions, The Catalyst for Health Care Reform, Washington DC: Deloitte Center for Health Solutions; 2006.

33. The Center for Responsive Politics. Lobbying Database, Washington DC: The Center for Responsive Politics; 2008. http://www.opensecrets.org/lobbyists/.

34. Consumer Union, Nonprofit Publisher of Consumers Report, The Statin Drugs: Prescription and Price Trends, November 2004 to October 2005.

35. GlobalSecutity.org: 2008

www.ingramcontent.com/pod-product-compliance
Lightning Source LLC
Chambersburg PA
CBHW061400280526
45784CB00001B/322